Foscolo Family of Venice Patricians and Aristocrats (A Genealogy)

Dr Mike P. Foscolos

Singapore, 2024

All rights reserved. No part of this publication may be reproduced, stored in a retrieval system, or in any form or by any means, without the prior permission in writing of the author, nor be otherwise circulated in any form of binding or cover other than that in which it is published and without a similar condition including this condition being imposed on the subsequent purchasers.

Singapore National Library cataloguing-in-publication data:

A catalogue record for this book is available from

The Singapore National Library

All pictures reproduced are in the public domain or are reproduced with the kind permission of the author.

ISBN: 978-981-18-3507-0

Copyright © 2024 M. P. Foscolos

All rights reserved.

Dedication

To all members of the Foscolo family past and present.

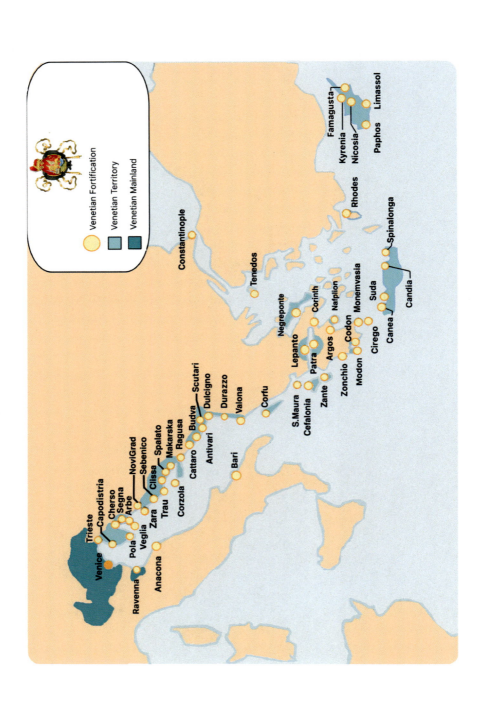

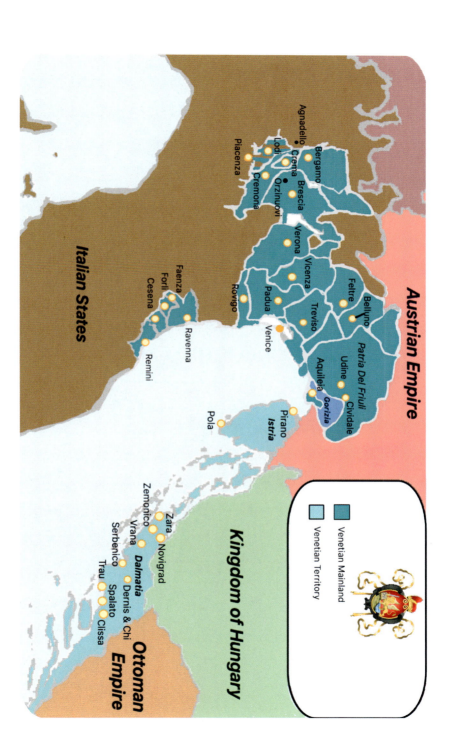

CONTENTS

Chapter 1 EARLY HISTORY 1
Family origins 1
Venetian nobility & succession 4
Medieval Branches 11

Chapter 2 REPUBLIC OF VENICE 16
14th – 15th Century 16
15th – 16th Century 30
16th - 17th Century 56
17th – 18th Century 73
18th – 19th Century 100
Ionian Islands Sub-Branch of Poet Ugo Foscolo 106

Chapter 3 POST REPIUBLIC OF VENCIE 110
The Kingdom of Lombardy-Venezia 117
The Kingdom of Italy 121

Chapter 4 LEVANT SUB-BRANCH 123
Life in the Levant 123
The 1922 Greek-Turkish Wars 133

Chapter 5 TITLES AND HERALDRY 141
Titles 141
Heraldry 143

FOREWORD

It has often been thought that the Foscolo family were one of the golden families, which founded the Republic of Venice in 423AD. While this may be debatable, there can be no doubt the family was one of the houses that made up the patriciate class, which ruled Venice until its fall in 1797. Despite the family's prominence, there have been few attempts to document its members and their historical contribution. This is hardly surprising. Although all political and economic power in Venice was vested in the patriciate, they acted as a collective. Each member of the patriciate was elected by their peers to serve in various judicial, administrative, and political offices. While the Republic maintained excellent records, to avoid corrupt practices patricians occupied state offices for only a short period of time (anywhere between 3 months to 5 years), before being elected to an entirely new post. This makes the contribution of individual patricians and their families extremely fractured and buried deep in the historical record.

The study of patrician families and their contributions to history requires a very granular approach, involving both genealogical tracing and careful analysis of antecedent history. Unlike stand-alone historical accounts or genealogical investigations, the nexus between the antecedent history and the genealogy is difficult to isolate. For this reason, a body of work that can holdup to academic scrutiny in terms of completeness and accuracy can only be achieved progressively over a significant length of time.

The earliest attempt to document the Foscolo family, and other families within the patriciate, is credited to Venetian historian and genealogist Marco Barbaro. In his work *Genealogie Patrizie,* he presents a crude genealogical tracing of each patrician family, together with a brief outline of each family's historical contribution. It was not until 1842 that Venetian writer and genealogist Emmanuele Cicogna produced the first genealogical tracing of the Foscolo family with antecedent history. His work takes the form of a letter entitled *"In the Marriage of the Nobleman Daulo Augusto Foscolo to the Baroness Margh Degli Orefic"*. Using Barbaro as a framework, he updates the genealogy of the family and adds antecedent history, largely sourced from notable Venetian historians Marino Sanuto (the elder and younger), Alessandro Cappellari, and Flaminio Conaro. This now published work was originally commissioned by Daulo Augustine Foscolo in support of his marriage into the noble Orefic family. Although many historians and genealogist question the completeness of the work, it was a significant step in producing an account of the Foscolo family and its historical contributions.

The author of this book has attempted to build on the work of Barboro and Cicogna, using the much richer body of literature now available, as well as historical records and manuscripts. He provides a much more accurate and complete genealogy of the Foscolo family and adds significantly to the antecedent history. This allows a more complete picture of the family's contribution to the Republic of Venice to emerge. More interestingly the book extends beyond the fall of the Republic of Venice and covers members of the family in the immediate aftermath, including the famous Italian nationalist and poet Ugo Foscolo. The book also traces a branch of the family to the Levant, providing a specific example to a question that has intrigued many; what happened to the Venetian Patricians in the aftermath of the Republic.

As historian and archivist of a noble branch of the Foscolo family, the author has been in a unique position, having benefited from contact with family members that held aristocratic title under the Kingdom of Italy, and who were themselves in contact with family members with first-hand knowledge of events as far back as the

Kingdom of Lombardy Venetia.

The author does not in any way presume this book provides a complete account. As with all historical and genealogical works, it stands to reason this body of work will be extended as new knowledge and information comes to hand. However, the book does represent significant progress on previous publications, and should be of interest to historians, genealogists, as well as those bearing the Foscolo name.

CHAPTER 1 EARLY HISTORY

Family origins

The name Foscolo is thought to derive from the Latin *fuscus*, meaning person of dark complexion. Some scholars chronicle the origin of the family to a Ugo Foscolo, who was thought to be a member of the golden families (*Aurelii*) who moved from Rome to build the Rialto of Venice between 423AD and 424AD.[1] Others believe the family's origins began with a Pietro Foscolo in 561AD, or from a Foscolo who offered tribunes in Torcello Venice in 570AD. Yet another account has the family originating from a Foscolo who offered tribunes in Grado Venice in 609AD.[2] The most credible of all accounts, has the Foscolo family originating from the Castle of Monselice, Piemonte, from where they moved to Malamocco Venice, before reaching the Rialto around 960AD.[3]

The Foscolo family was described in chronicles from the Middle Ages[4] as *"homeni di bona conscientia benivoli et amadori della sua patria"*, of good conscience, benevolent, and loving of their country. "No less rich than religious", the family was credited with contributing to the building of the church of San Marco di Boccalama in 1122. The church was found on the border of the Venice marshes facing the Padua countryside. After 1328, subsidence and erosion made life impossible for the monks, and by 1348 it was used only as a burial ground during outbreaks of

---

[1] Cavaccia, J: Aula Zabarella Hugo Fuscus Familiae Fusculae originem dedisse agunt, I. de Cadorinis, 1670, pp. 102, 104
[2] Vaggassi l'opera: Delle Montete dei Veneziani, Part 1, 1818, pp. 27, 28, 29, 98, 107
[3] Cicogna, E: Nelle Nozze Dell Nobile Daulo Augusto Di Foscolo Colla Baronessa Margh Degli Orefic, 1842, p. 2
[4] ibid, p. 2

The Castle of Monselice, Piemonte

Location of the Castle of Monselice, Google Maps

Early History

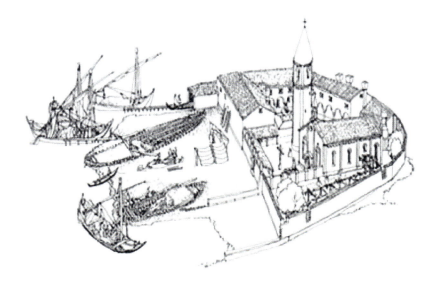

San Marco di Boccalama, anonymous sketch

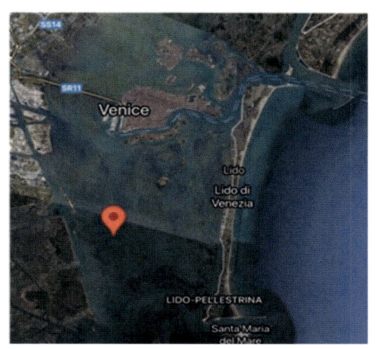

Location of San Marco di Boccalama, **Google Maps**

the plague. The last mentions of San Marco di Boccalama date to the 16th century, after which time it most likely completely submerged.[5]

Venetian nobility & succession

Although the Foscolo family was settled in Venice as early as 960AD, had contributed to the building of San Marco di Boccalama in 1122, and was chronicled as a wealthy and respected family, this did not in itself qualify it as nobility. Venetian society was stratified into three social groups: Patricians, Citizens, and Foreigners. Patricians were the aristocracy of the Venetian Republic. Their power was not based on the possession of land, but on the total control of political and economic influence in the state.

At the time the Foscolo family arrived in Venice, political power rested with the General Assembly of Men (*Conico*), from which the head of state (*Doge*) was elected, and with whom the Doge consulted on matters of state. It was at this time that the Patrician class had its genesis. Prominent families sought a place on the General Assembly of Men, to influence and direct politics. In 1143, the Council of Wise Men[6] (*Consilium Sapientium*), was established to oversee government. This council consisted of both citizens and members of the prominent families, who were appointed by the Doge.

Thirty years later in 1172, the Consilium Sapientium and Conico

---

5 Marsilio editori, La galea ritrovata Origine delle cose di Venezia, a cura di Consorzio Venezia Nuova, 2002
6 Armstrong, L and Kirshner, J: The Politics of Law in Late Medieval and Renaissance Italy, U Toronto Press, 2011, pp. 40-55

were absorbed into an assembly known as the Great Council[7] (*Maggior Consiglio*). Unlike previous councils of state, members of the Great Council were no longer directly appointed by the Doge but were elected by members of the Council itself. Most members of the Council were elected to serve in various offices and magistracy's, which performed all judicial, financial, and administrative functions of State. A subset of the Great Council was elected by members to serve in the Senate (*Pregardi*). This was one of the most powerful bodies in the Republic. It was entrusted with all law-making activities and was responsible for foreign affairs and trade. Forty experienced members of the Great Council were elected by members to another powerful body, the Council of Forty (*Quarantia*).[8] This acted as a Supreme Court of Appeal and was responsible for coinage and finances. In later years, the Council of Forty was also responsible for electing the head of state (*Doge*) for his life term. Ten experience members of the Great Council were elected by members to serve on the much-feared Council of Ten. This body was created in 1310 and was responsible for state security. It was aimed at protecting the government from overthrow and corruption, akin to modern-day intelligence service. It had both inquisitorial and enforcement powers. Standing apart from all other state offices, it had secret funds, a network of anonymous informers, judicial and police powers.[9] The Doge was at the top of the power structure as quasi head of state, followed by six Ducal Councillors, which together proposed and authorised policies, in the same manner as a -

---

[7] Lane, F: Venice, a maritime republic, Johns Hopkins U Press, 1973, p. 112
[8] Diehl, C: La Repubblica di Venezia, Newton & Compton editori, Roma, 2004
[9] Iordanou, I: The Spy Chiefs of Renaissance Venice: Intelligence Leadership in the Early Modern World, Spy Chiefs, Volume 2, Georgetown U Press, 2018, pp. 43-66

Foscolo Family of Venice: Patricans and Aristocrats (A Genealogy)

Great Council, Joseph Heintz Younger (1600-1678)

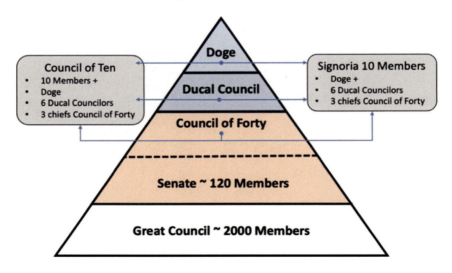

The Structure of Government, Republic of Venice.

modern-day cabinet ministry. Later in 1423 the Doge and Ducal Councillors were joined by the three Chiefs of the Council of Forty and became known collectively as the Signoria.[10] In addition to policy making, the signoria was always present at meetings of the Council of Ten. In effect, the Venetian Republic was a form of constitutional monarchy, with members of the Great Council overseeing and participating in all three arms of government, namely: legislative, administrative, and judicial.

Although the patrician class (consisting of the old and prominent families) were dominant in the Great Council, their emergence as a hereditary aristocracy was cemented by the Great Council Lockout of 1297 [11] (*Serrata del Maggior Consiglio*). This ordinance ruled that only persons having served as a member of the Great Council in the previous four years or paternally related to a former member, could become a member of the Great Council. As a result, membership of the Great Council became a hereditary right, limited to a few prominent families. Citizens and newer families were excluded from participating in all three branches of government. This concentration of political and economic power into the hands of a few old and prominent families, led to the formalisation of the Patriciate, a form of aristocracy, which ruled Venice as an oligarchy.

As part of the Patriciate, the Foscolo family were prominent in Councils of State. Flamingo Cornaro [12] noted that the family despite having been in Venice since 965AD, was not accepted in the Councils until 1267. Furthermore, according to genealogist

---

10 Queller, E: The Venetian Patriciate: Reality versus Myth, Chicago of University of Illinois Press, 1986, p. 347'
11 Lane, F: Venice, a maritime republic, Johns Hopkins University Press, 1973
12 Flaminio Conaro: Ecces Ven, vi, 78 e seg. xi, 88, 91 xiv, p. 306

Marco Barbaro,[13] the family's ascension only occurred after it favoured unpopular policies proposed by the Doge and Government. This seems to cast a shadow on the prominence of the family, at least in its early years. However, these accounts seem to lack credibility, as there is a great deal of evidence to suggest the Foscolo family were involved in councils of state much earlier. The diary of Sanuto[14] tells of the renovations to the fortress of Loredo in 1094 under Doge Vital Faliero. Each family were obliged to supply three chickens, seven eels, and three deniers per year, as tribute for the work undertaken. A solemn pact was made bearing the signature of the Doge Pietro Badoaro the patriarch of Grado, two judges, and many others, one of whom was a Dom Nico Foscolo. Notably, all signatories to the pact were not taken from the class of "artisans and low people", but persons of "good and older families".[15] In 1122, a Pietro Foscolo subscribed to an important instrument made with the community of Bari, in which the Doge Michiel swears never to allow anyone from Bari to lose his life or substance through the fault of the Venetians.[16] This was an important document, signed only by high level nobles. A security charter of 1151 issued to Pietro and Giovanni Basegio de Danari, bears signature of the Doge, co-judges, and 249 nobles including a Marco Foscolo.[17] Cappellari[18] noted in 1192, a Foscolo was one of the electors of Doge Enrico Dandolo.[19] In 1205, Stefano Foscolo was one of the

---

13 Cicogna, E: Nelle Nozze Dell Nobile Daulo Augusto Di Foscolo Colla Baronessa Margh Degli Orefic, 1842, p. 7
14 Sanuto, R. I. S. tom xxii, p. 479
15 Cicogna (n13), p. 7
16 Sanuto, (n14), p. 966
17 Inscriz Veneziane, vol iv, p. 563
18 Cappellari, Alessandro nel Campidoglio Venito Codice della Marciana
19 Sanuto, (n14), p. 527

electors of Doge Pietro Ziani.[20] The historical record shows, overwhelmingly, that the Foscolo family's ascendance to councils of state occurred much earlier than 1267. In fact, from the early part of the 11th Century the family participated in affairs of state.

Crucially, the Foscolo family retained their membership of the Great Council following the lockout of 1297. In 1315, shortly after the lockout, those families who received a hereditary right of inclusion in the Great Council were codified in the golden book (*Libro d'Oro*). Four families were registered in the golden book as old houses, *case vecchie*.[21] These were the most prestigious families, noted for electing the first Doge in 697AD.[22] One hundred and fifty two families were registered as new houses, *case nuove*.[23] Although of medieval origin, and no less significant in stature, these families did not have the antiquity and therefore prestige of the older houses. In later additions of the golden book, from 1379, an entirely new category of families appear, the brand-new houses, *casa novísimas*.[24] Thirty families made significant financial contributions to the Republic's war efforts and were honoured with hereditary right of inclusion in the Great Council. These brand-new houses were known colloquially as *houses made for a penny*, as their nobility was purchased. The Foscolo family were recorded in the first golden book in 1315 as a new house, *case nuove*,[25] and remained in the book until the end of the Venetian Republic in 1797. On this basis alone, there can be

---

20 Sanuto, R. I. S. tom xxii, P 535, Dandalo R. I. S. tom xii, P. 345
21 ibid
22 Maschietto, F: Elena Lucrezia Cornaro Piscopia (1646-1684): prima donna laureata nel mondo, Antenore, 1978, p. 4
23 Chojnacki, S: La formazione della nobiltà dopo la Serrata, in Storia di Venezia, Vol. 3, Treccani, 1997
24 ibid
25 ibid

no doubt that the Foscolo family were a preeminent family early in the Republics history.

All direct descendants of patricians had a hereditary right of membership in the Great Council, but it was not without condition. To be a member of the Great Council, and enjoy privileges of nobility, one had to be registered in the golden book. Laws were passed placing conditions on registration in this book. As early as 1276, bastards were prohibited from admission into the Great Council. This was reaffirmed in 1376, when only legitimate descendants of Patricians were permitted to be registered in the golden book.[26] Further conditions were imposed in the 14th Century, when Patricians were restricted in marriage to women who were the daughters of nobles, doctors, goldsmiths, glass blowers, grocers, and women from equally respectable families.[27] Recording of noble births began in September 1506 and recording of noble marriages began in January 1526.[28] Morganatic descendants, that is offspring of Patricians who married women of a lower social standing, were prohibited from registering in the golden book. Even if a Patrician married acceptably, and their offspring was legitimately conceived within wedlock, their offspring's hereditary right of membership in the Great Council, and their nobility, was only conferred once their parents' marriage and their birth was registered in the golden book.

---

[26] Crescenzi, V: Stern Laura Ikins review of Esse de maiori consilio: Leggittimita civile e legittimazione politica nella repubblica di Venezia (secc. XIII-XVI), The American Journal of Legal History XLII, 1998, pp. 289-291

[27] McClellan, G. B: Venice and Bonaparte, Literary Licensing LLC, 2011, pp. 48-49

[28] ibid

Medieval Branches

Although members of the Foscolo family can be traced back to 10th Century Venice, their descendants are not considered noble unless it can be shown there were registered in the golden book. It is possible for entire branches of the family to lose their nobility over time as proceeding generations failed to register their marriages and/or offspring. These branches include the medieval branches of the family, which split from the noble branch in the 11th Century. The split followed the Fourth Crusade, a joint expedition undertaken by the Franks and the Republic, with the noble intention of freeing Jerusalem from the Muslim infidels.

The objective of the Fourth Crusade was to defeat the powerful Egyptian Ayyubid Sultanate. As it turned out, instead of proceeding to Egypt as planned, a series of economic and political events led the crusaders to sack Constantinople in 1204. This led to the Byzantine Empire being partition between the Crusaders, and the short-lived Latin Emperor of Constantinople they enthroned.[29,30]

The Republic under Doge Enrico Dandalo was the greatest beneficiary of the partition, receiving three eights of the Byzantine Empire. However, it was a division on paper only. Many of the imperial possessions had Byzantine officials in control and needed to be taken by force.

Candia (modern day Crete) was allotted to the Frank, Boniface of Montferrate, but being unable to enforce his control over the island, he sold it to the Republic for 1000 marks of silver in

---

[29] Norwich, J: Byzantium:Decline and Fall, London, Penguin Books, 1995, P169
[30] Morris, J:The Venetian Empire:A SeaVoyage, Penguine, 1990

1205.[31] In the same year the newly elected Doge Pietro Ziani, decided to offer the Cyclades Islands to free enterprise. Any Venetian citizens with enough ships and men were permitted to take the islands for themselves as feudal chiefs, provided of course they remained loyal to the Republic. The challenge was taken up by the nephew of the recently deceased Doge Enrico Dandolo, Marin Sanudo. Equipped with eight fighting galleys, he seized the Cyclades Island and declared himself Duke of Naxos. True to his promise, Sanudo divided some of the islands among his five noble companions. One of these companions was a Leonardo Foscolo who received the Island of Naphomi (Anafi), declaring himself Lord. [32,33]

The Foscolo family ruled the island of Anafi for close to a century over three generations: Leonardo Foscolo (1207 to 1252), Andrea Foscolo (1252 to 1278), and John Foscolo (1278 to 1296). Many wrongly believe the Foscolo family of the Cyclades gave rise to the many branches of the family that flourished across the Aegean by the end of the 15th Century. However, in 1296 Anafi native and Genovese pirate, John de lo Cavo, whilst serving as Megas Doux of the Byzantine Navy, recovered the island of Anafi on behalf of Byzantine Emperor Micheal VIII Palaeologos. John Foscolo was deposed as Lord of Anafi, and all members of the Foscolo family were expelled from the island.[34] Following this event there is no mention of the Foscolo family of the Cyclades or their descendants. The many medieval sub-branches of the Foscolo family that emerged across the Aegean, most likely hail from the

---

[31] Miller, W: The Latins in the Levant: A History of Frankish Greece (1204–1566), John Murray, London, 1908 p 29
[32] Morris, J:The Venetian Empire:A SeaVoyage, Penguine, 1990
[33] Miller (n31), p 44
[34] ibid, p 578

Candian branch, which also had its genesis shortly after the Fourth Crusade.

Shortly after the partition of the Byzantine Empire, the Republic enforced its claim over Candia (modern day Crete). In 1205 a small force was landed on Spinalonga. At the time the Genovese had a small trading colony on the island under the command of adventurer, Enrico Pescatore, Count of Malta. Under his leadership the local Greek population resisted Venetian rule. It would not be until 1212 that the Republic gain full control of the island.[35]

To help secure Candia the first Governor, Giacomo Tiopolo (*Duca di Candia*), called for colonists to be sent from Venice, and suggested land be offered in exchange for military service. His suggestion was approved by the Senate and a Charter was proclaimed in Venice in 1211 (*Carta Concessioni*). The first wave of Venetian colonists arrived in Candia in 1212 comprising of 132 nobles, who were to serve as knights, and 45 citizens.[36] Amongst these colonists were two noble brothers, Leonardo, and Giovanni Foscolo, who had been living in the district of San Croce Venice.[37] As per the Charter, Giacomo Tiepolo divided the castles, villas, and lands in Candia between the Venetian colonists. The colonists appointed a "prudent and expert patrician", *Capitanîo*, to represent their respective district of Venice during the division. The *Capitanîo* representing the colonists from the district of San Croce was the said Leonardo.[38] Since that time multiple sub-

---

[35] Detorakis, T, E: Ιστορία της Κρήτης [History of Crete, Athens, 1986 pp 164-165
[36] Ibid, pp 166-167
[37] Muazzo, G. A: Cronico famiglie nobili Venete andate in Candia, MSS
[38] Cornaro, A: Storia di Candia, Creta sacra ii, p. 237, MSS

branches of the Foscolo family appeared on the island.[39]

As early as 1230, there is mention of a Foscolo family of Candia, who in 1272 fought valiantly to aid the Republic quell a rebellion. This rebellion occurred when several families on the island revolted against Venetian domination, including the noble Greek family led by brothers George and Theodore Chortatzes. The rebels engaged the Venetian army led by Marino Zeno on the Messara Plain. There was significant loss of life, including two members of the Foscolo family of Candia.[40] In 1252, there is also mention of an Enrico Foscolo from a separate Santa Apostolo sub-branch of the family,[41] and by the time of the last Candian War in the 15th Century, there were many sub-branches of the Foscolo family on Candia, whose members "had neglected their nobility, but lived civilly".[42]

The descendants of these medieval branches of the Foscolo family, share a common ancestry, but do not share in its nobility. Many of those whose names have been Hellenized to Foskolos, and many of the Ottoman-Latino Catholics baring the name Foscolo, are descended from these ancient branches of the family. **Marco Antonio Foskolos (1597 - 1662)**, the famous Greek playwright, hails from the Candian branch of the family.[43] It has also been suggested that the famous 18th Century poet Ugo Foscolo, may have descended from this branch of the family, with his ancestors moving from Candia to Corfu in the 15th Century. However, there is a great deal of evidence to support the great poet descended from a noble branch of the family, which lost its

---

39 Cornaro, A: Storia di Candia, Creta sacra ii,, pp. 237,238
40 Muazzo, G. A: Cronico famiglie nobili Venete andate in Candia, MSS
41 Corano, A: Storia di Candia, Creta Sacra ii, MSS, pp. 237,238
42 ibid
43 Established from the marriage contract of his parents, dated April 12, 1595

nobility at a much later time.44 This will be discussed further in Chapter 2.

---

44 Gemelli, C: Della Vita Delle Opere Di Ugo Foscolo, Firenze, 1849 pp. 60-61

CHAPTER 2 REPUBLIC OF VENICE

This chapter is concerned with those members of the Foscolo family who were Venetian Patricians, and whose descendants were subsequently conferred hereditary aristocratic title at the end of the 18th Century. Genealogical tracing of these noble branches of the family begins in 1297, as kinship connections before this time are uncertain. The Foscolo family lineage as recorded by notable Venetian historian Marco Barboro[45] is used as a framework. This is complemented by information recorded in various editions of the golden book, commentaries from the 18th Century Venetian genealogist and writer Emmanuele Cicogna,[46] public records, and historical manuscripts. The focus is on the male hereditary line and follows the Foscolo family tree (1255 to 1797) shown below.

14th – 15th Century

The noble Foscolo lineage begins with an **Almorà Foscolo (1252-1316)**, son of Andrea, who lived in the district of San Vio Venice. Following the lockout of 1297, he took his place in the Great Council. [47] The lineage progresses to the grandson of Almorà, **Andrea Foscolo (1314-1365)**, son of Francesco. In 1349 he was serving on a specially formed council of three wise men, tasked with resolving a long running civil dispute between the widow of Rizzardo da Camino the exiled Lord of Treviso, and his heirs.[48]

---

[45] Nobiltà veneta con le arme et insegne di cadauna famiglia, Volume III, 1725
[46] Cicogna, E: Nelle Nozze Dell Nobile Daulo Augusto Di Foscolo Colla Baronessa Margh Degli Orefic, 1842 p. 10
[47] Sanuto, R. I. S. tom xxii, p. 636
[48] Senato Mis, register 25, folio 27r, 1349

Republic of Venice

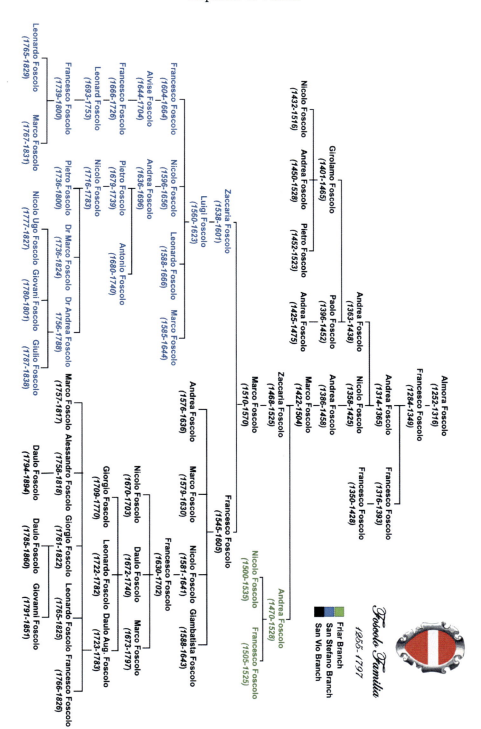

On the death of Rizzardo III da Camino, son of Geuecellone VII, in 1324, his widow who had him build a mausoleum in San Giustina in Serravalle, received an inheritance on behalf of his daughters Caterina, Beatrice and Rizzarda. However, the male heirs of the da Camino family, Gherardo and Rizzardo, contested the inheritance, leading to a long running highly publicised dispute.[49] Andrea with two other Patricians were tasked with judging this high-profile civil matter.[50]

In 1351 Andrea Foscolo was elected Governor of Negroponte (*Provveditore Negroponte*).[51,] This was an important position at the time as in the previous year, 1350, the Third Venetian Genovese War had begun. Genoa had captured a force of Venetian galleys which were anchored at the port of Caffa on Crimea in the Black Sea. The Republic sent an emissary to demand an explanation and reparations from the Genovese, but the request was ignored. As a result, the two powers went to war. The Venetian fleet under Marco Ruzzini, captured ten Genovese vessels in the harbour at Negroponte. Despite this gain, through incompetence, four ships were allowed to escape to the Genovese Island of Chios. On their arrival in Chios, they joined forces with nine other galleys, sailed back to Negroponte, and inflicted a great deal of damage. The Genovese gained control of the port, looted the city, and captured some twenty Venetian merchant ships, which were docked in the harbour.[52] It was by pure good fortune

---

49 Enrica, A & Bongi, P:Sulle terre dei da Camino, Pieve da Soligo:Bubola & Naibo, 1993
50 Riedmann, J: CAMINO, Rizzardo da, Dizionario Biografico degli Italiani - Volume 17, 1974
51 Senato Secreta, folio 34v, 1352
52 Norwich, J Venice, The Rise to Empire. London; Penguin Books, 1978, p.240

Citadel at Negroponte, Giacomo Franco 1597

Harbour and Venetian Tower at Negroponte

that the Venetian troops in the citadel were able to maintain control of the island. Following this debacle, both Marco Ruzzini and the Governor of Negroponte, Tommaso Viadro, faced trial by the Council of Ten. Although both were acquitted, they never again held military office. It was in the immediate aftermath of this fiasco that Andrea Foscolo was dispatched as Governor of Negroponte. On his arrival he immediately set about repairing damage to the port and fortifications and prepared for an imminent attack by the Genovese. A second attack came in late 1351. Nicolo Pisani the newly elected Commander of the Venetian Navy (*Capitanîo Generale da Mar*), received communications informing him a large Genovese fleet led by Paganino Doria was headed to Negroponte. He quickly headed for the ravaged port. On arrival he sank his galleys in the harbour to protect them from Doria's fleet, and together with Andrea Foscolo prepared the defences of the island. When the Genovese fleet arrived at Negroponte, the Venetians put up fierce resistance, and the Genovese fleet was successfully repelled, withdrawing to Pera (a city close to Constantinople).[53,54]

On his return from Negroponte, Andrea Foscolo was elected Governor of Montona in Istria (*Pòdesta di Montona*).[55] At the end of his term Andrea was elected to the Council of Forty, where he was an elector of Doge Giovanni Gradenigo in 1355.[56] In the same year, Genoa and the Republic signed a peace treaty ending the Third Genovese-Venetian War. However, peace in the

---

[53] Balard, M: Dal trattato di Milano al 1345. La lotta contro Genova, stituto dell'Enciclopedia Italiana, 2021

[54] Lane, F: Venice and History: The Collected Papers of Frederic C. Lane, Baltimore, The Johns Hopkins Press, 1966, p176

[55] Segretario alle Voci, register 1, folio, 53v, 1352

[56] Sanuto, R. I. S. tom xxii, p. 636

Republic did not last long.

In 1356 following a dispute with Venice over territory in Dalmatia, King Lajos of Hungary seized control of all Venetian territory on the eastern shores of the Adriatic and led his troops into Friuli. The King wisely approached neighbouring Padua to break its peace agreement with Venice and join in the struggle. Despite the lack of Paduan support, King Lajos enjoyed some success, with Venetian mainland towns of Conegliano and Sacile falling to the advancing Hungarian army. Padua eventually gave King Lajos support, with the Hungarians gaining Sarravalle and Asolo before laying siege to the town of Treviso.[57] As war with the Hungarians raged on the mainland, Andrea Foscolo was serving as Governor of Cordon *(Rettore Castellano di Cordone)* a fortification in Morea (modern day Peloponnese).[58] He returned to Venice in 1357 and was elected to the Council of Ten.[59] This was an eventful time for Andrea and other members of the council. Its actions helped thwart a defection plot by Treviso, which would have seen the city capitulate to the Hungarians without a fight. Later that year, Andrea Foscolo was elected to the council of five wise men of war *(Savi di Guerra)*,[60] a special council formed by the Senate to oversee the war effort against the Hungarians.[61] Following his appointment, Venetian troops were sent to attack Padua with little success, and defences were readied on the mainland.[62] In the Spring of 1357, the Hungarian army launched an attack on Venetian possessions on the mainland with

---

[57] Norwich, J: A History of Venice, Paperback, 18 June 1989, p. 256
[58] Senato Misti, Register 27, folio 227v, 1356
[59] Sanuto, R. I. S. tom xxii, p. 653
[60] Senato Misti Register 28 folio 17r,1357
[61] Cicogna, E: Nelle Nozze Dell Nobile Daulo Augusto Di Foscolo Colla Baronessa Margh Degli Orefic,1842, p. 10
[62] Sanuto (n59)

Castelfranco, Oderzo, and Treviso all successfully defended. However, the situation in Treviso remained precarious, and King Lajos steadily gained control of the shores of the lagoon.[63] Andrea Foscolo and other members of the Council hastily prepared for the defence of the City of Venice.[64] However, the Hungarian invaders had clearly advanced to a point where they were threatening the very existence of the Republic. As a result, the recently elected Doge Dolphin, despite calls to resist the Hungarians at all costs, had little choice but to find a diplomatic solution. In February 1358 a peace treaty was signed with Hungary, with the Republic ceding much of its territory in Dalmatia.[65]

In 1361, Andrea Foscolo was serving on the Council of Forty, where he was an elector of Doge Lorenzo Celsi.[66] Shortly after the election, he was appointed to serve on the council of twelve wise men for Treviso (*Savi di Treviso*).[67] A special council formed to act as arbiter and peacemaker in the disputes that had arisen between Treviso and the Republic during the Hungarian war. Later that year, presumably given his position on the council and his knowledge of the situation in Treviso, Andrea Foscolo was elected as Governor of Treviso (*Provveditore di Treviso*).[68]

At the end of 1362 Andrea Foscolo was elected Ambassador to Constantinople (*Bailo Constantinopli*).[69] His appointment came

---

63 Norwich, J: A History of Venice, Paperback, 18 June 1989, p. 256
64 Sanuto, R. I. S. tom xxii, p. 653
65 Mark, R.F: Venetian Foreign Affairs from 1250 to 1381: The Wars with Genoa and Other External Developments, U Illinois, 1988 pp.71-72
66 Sanuto (n64)
67 Senato Misti, register 30, folio 44r, 1361
68 Senato Misti, register 30, folio, 35r, 1361
69 Segretario Voci Register 2, folio,23r, 1363

following two Byzantine civil wars, which saw John V Paleologos in 1357 succeed in his struggle to become the sole Byzantine Emperor. A few years earlier John V had ascended to the throne at the age of eight under a council of regents. This council was composed of his mother Anna of Savoy, the patriarch John XIV Kalekas, and the Megas Doux Alexios Apokaukos. A civil war immediately broke out when John VI Katakouzinos, a friend of John V's father, declared himself regent. To fund the first civil war John V's mother pawned the Byzantine crown jewels to the Republic in exchange for a loan of 30,000 ducats. The first civil war was lost to John VI Katakouzinos, who from 1347 ruled as co-Emperor. However, in the second civil war John V retook Constantinople in 1354, and finally deposed John VI Katakouzinos in 1357. However, victory for John V did not come cheap. On his arrival in Constantinople Andrea Foscolo was instructed by the Senate to seek audience with the Byzantine Emperor John V, and demand settlement of his large debt to the Republic.[70,71]

On his return to Venice late in 1363, Andrea Foscolo was appointed one of the wise men over matters relating to the Emperor of Constantinople (*Savi dell Imperatore di Costantinopoli*).[72] This special council was formed by the Senate to pose solutions to John V's ballooning debt. It set the stage for Emperor John V to be famously detained as a debtor in Venice in October 1369 at the time of his Imperial visit. It was at this time that John V offered the Island of Tenedos to the Republic in exchange for cancelling 20,000 ducats of his debt and the return

---

[70] Nicol, D. M.: Bizantium and Venice: A study in cultural and deplomatic relations, Cambridge University Press, 1988
[71] Harris, J: The End of Byzantium, Yale University Press, 2010
[72] Senato Misti, register 31, folio 52v, 1363

of his crown jewels. It was not until 1376 that the island of Tenedos was finally sold to the Republic for 20,000 ducats in partial fulfilment of the debt.[73] Andrea Foscolo did not live to see the partial settlement, as he died around 1365 and was survived by his sons Nicolo and Andrea.

At the same time as Andrea, lived his brother **Francesco Foscolo (1330-1393)**, who while sailing on a Venetian galley carrying rich merchandise was made a slave of the Corsairs. He managed to secure his freedom from slavery, and in 1372 was part of a delegation of four Venetian Patricians who met with the Ambassador to the Duke of Padua Francesco da Carrara.[74] The meeting held at the monastery of San Georgia Maggiore, was to negotiate a settlement following Padua's decision to build a salt production facility. This was interpreted as an affront by the Republic, which held a century old monopoly on salt production and distribution in the region. Hungary acted as a facilitator at the talks, with the Venetian position being that Padua should stop salt production voluntarily. The negotiations failed, and the disagreement quickly escalated into a military confrontation. The Republic contracted the mercenary Renier del Gauschi to lead its troops, and quickly attacked Padua and besieged the city. The Duke of Padua in response hatched a scheme to assassinate several leaders of the Republic with the help of two traitorous members of the Senate.[75] At this time, in 1373, Francesco Foscolo was one of the three Chiefs of the Council of Ten, which had

---

[73] Nicol, D.M.: The Reluctant Emperor: A Biography of John Cantacuzene, Byzantine Emperor and Monk, c. 1295-1383, Cambridge University Press, 1996

[74] Cicogna, E: Nelle Nozze Dell Nobile Daulo Augusto Di Foscolo Colla Baronessa Margh Degli Orefic,1842, p. 10

[75] Hazlitt, W. C.: The Venetian Republic: Its Rise. Its Growth, and Its Fall 421-1797 Nabu (first published 1900), 2011 pp.686,687

responsibility for subversion against the Republic.[76] The plot was discovered by the Council, and news of the murderous plans caused a great deal of fear and anger in Venice. Francesco Foscolo and other members of the Council of Ten metered harsh punishment to the two nobles who were plotting with Francesco da Carrara, with one being beheaded and the other imprisoned for ten years. The two assassins who had agreed to work for the nobles were publicly drawn and quartered.[77]

In 1378, Francesco Foscolo was on a Venetian galley headed for Cyprus. He was leading a delegation of six Venetian nobles accompanying Valentina daughter of Bernabò Visconti, Lord of Milan. She was to be married by proxy to King Peter II the fat of Cyprus.[78] King Peter II had been crowned in Nicosia in 1372. During the crowning ceremony in Famagusta leaders of the Genovese and Venetian communities, in accordance with custom, were given the honour of holding the two reins of the royal horse. There was a disagreement over who would hold the right rein and who would hold the left. This conflict grew and continued into the celebration dinner, and afterward spilled on to the streets of Famagusta. Venetians and the Genovese fought each other, resulting in a great deal of damage. The Genovese were considered responsible for the fighting and were arrested. In Genoa the news of the arrests was not well received. They felt their diplomats had been treated unfairly, and were victims of discriminatory justice. Motivated in part by a fear the Republic was gaining control of Cyprus, which had the potential to

---

[76] Consiglio dei Dieci, Mis, register 6, folio 123r, 1373
[77] Hazlitt, W. C.: The Venetian Republic: Its Rise. Its Growth, and Its Fall 421-1797 Nabu (first published 1900), 2011 pp.686, 687
[78] Cicogna, E: Nelle Nozze Dell Nobile Daulo Augusto Di Foscolo Colla Baronessa Margh Degli Orefic,1842, p.10

seriously harm Genovese trade interests in the east, they sent a military expedition capturing Famagusta, then attacking Limassol and Paphos, before entering the Kingdom's Capital Nicosia. The following year in 1374, King Peter II was forced to come to a humiliating agreement with the Genovese, declaring Kyrenia, and what remained of Famagusta Genovese sovereignty.[79] This incident in Cyprus, as well as tensions arising from the Republics gain of the Island of Tenedos from the Byzantines, as partial settlement for the debt owed to the Republic by Byzantine Emperor John V, led to the War of Chioggia 1378 to 1381, also known as the Fourth Venetian-Genovese War. Genoa had succeeded in bringing all the traditional enemies of Venice to her side, namely Padua, the Austrian Duchy, and the King of Hungary. The marriage of King Peter II to the daughter of the Duke of Milan facilitated an alliance between Milan, Cyprus, and Venice against Genoa in the war. During his time in Cyprus, it was Francesco Foscolo who in aid of King Peter II, attempted to recover Famagusta from the hands of the Genovese. Although his attempt was ultimately unsuccessful, it tied up Genovese resources at a critical time.[80]

Meanwhile in Venice war had started strongly for the Genovese, with the Venetian fleet suffering successive defeats at the Battles of Anzio and Pola, and the Genovese advancing as far as Chioggia directly threating the City of Venice itself. The Paduan forces closed in by land. However, the Venetian fleet in December 1379 had managed to mount a blockade of Chioggia, cutting Genovese supply lines and communications. By June 1380 the blockade forced four thousand Genovese and two hundred Paduans to

---

[79] Edbury, P: The Kingdom of Cyprus and the Crusades 1191–1374, Cambridge University Press, 1994
[80] Sanuto, R. I. S. tom xxii, p. 681

unconditionally surrender, and the Genovese Admiral to withdraw his fleet to the shores of Dalmatia.[81] Although the surrender at Chioggia was a significant turning point in the war, it did not mark its conclusion. Venice was suffering from shortages of many critical products. The Venetian Navy was pursuing and attempting to destroy the Genovese fleet. The battles with the Paduans on the mainland continued. An alliance was being concluded with the Duke of Austria who was switching his alliance from Padua to the Republic.[82] It was not until September 1381 that the peace treaty with the Genovese was signed in Turin. It required, amongst other things, the Republic abandon the contentious Island of Tenedos and raze its fortifications, and transfer Treviso to the Austrians, who would later sell it to Padua in 1382.[83]

In 1383 Francesco Foscolo was elected to the Supreme Consul of the Merchants *(Sopra Console dei Mercanti)*,[84] the magistracy responsible for judging bankruptcy petitions in Venice. Late in 1384 he was elected Consul to Damascus (*Console di Damasco*).[85]

Francesco Foscolo returned to the Senate in 1386, before being appointed to the powerful Ducal Council. His term on the Council began in December 1387.[86] This was a critical time. Padua under Francesco I da Carrara, had continued to pursue a policy of expansion after the War of Chioggia. Forming an alliance with Ferrara in the west, purchasing Treviso from the Dutchy of

---

[81] Mark, R.F: Venetian Foreign Affairs from 1250 to 1381: The Wars with Genoa and Other External Developments, U Illinois, 1988 pp.71-72
[82] ibid
[83] Senato Misti, Register 36, folio 103v, 1380
[84] Segretario Voci Register 3, folio 15r, 1387
[85] Segretario Voci Register 3, folio 32v, 1384
[86] Segretario Voci Register 3, folio 1r, 1387

Austria, and trying to gain influence with Friuli in the east, Padua had in effect encircled Venice and threatened to cut the Republics trade routes leading over the Alps to Germany. Francesco Foscolo together with other Ducal Councillors, made the decision to enter an alliance with the Duke of Milan Gian Galeazzo Visconti to counter Padua. This alliance succeeded, Francesco I da Carrara was forced to resign in 1388, and Venice gained control of Treviso.[87] Padua itself fell briefly to Milan, but in June 1390, with the backing of Florence and the support of Venice, the son of Francesco I da Carrara, Francesco II da Carrara, recovered control of Padua. During the following years, Padua reverted to being a useful buffer between the Republic and an expanding Milan.[88]

In April 1389 Francesco Foscolo, was dispatched to Constantinople.[89] At the time the Republic had failed to come to a satisfactory arrangement with the Byzantine Emperor John V, regarding settlement of his debt to Venice, and the renewal of a treaty governing the rights of Venetian Citizens in Constantinople. Andrea Bembo had been dispatched as Ambassador to Constantinople in 1389 and had returned to Venice empty handed. Five years earlier, Lodovico Contarini had been despatched and had evidently tried to bully the emperor in a tactless manner. In fact, John V had felt impelled to write twice to the Doge, Antonio Venier, to protest at Contarini's offensive and dishonest behaviour. It had been Contarini's fault that the customary treaty had not been confirmed in 1384 and was most

---

[87] Lane, F: *Venice, a maritime republic*, Johns Hopkins University Press, 1973 pp. 200, 226–227.226.
[88] Billanovich, G. & Chiara, M: *CARRARA, Francesco da, il Novello*, Dizionario Biografico degli Italiani, Vol 20: Carducci Carusi, Rome: Istituto dell Enciclopedia Italiana, 1977
[89] Senato Misti, Register 40, folio 166v, 1389

likely why the recent negotiations had failed. There was some doubt about what Francesco Foscolo would find when he got to Constantinople. The Emperor professed he had lost none of his love and friendship for Venice. However, these words belied the fact that the Venetians in Constantinople complained more and more about the injustices inflicted on them by the emperor's officials. There was also a family feud raging in Constantinople, and there was some doubt who would be Emperor on Francesco's arrival. Francesco Foscolo was instructed to seek audience with either John V or his grandson John VII depending on which of them was in power. In either case he was to issue an ultimatum to the effect; if no satisfaction was given and if difficulties were made about renewing the treaty, the Venetian merchants in Constantinople would be evacuated for their own safety. Ships would be at hand to take them to Negroponte. However, if Foscolo found that the Sultan Bayezid was in control of the city, he should temper his demands. Clearly the Venetians were expecting the Ottomans to march into Constantinople at any moment. Foscolo was lucky to reach Constantinople during the brief reign of John VII, for John gave him no trouble. Presumably on the grounds that he needed all the friends he could get. He lost no time in giving the Venetians all that they wanted without quibbling or prevaricating. The treaty which Venice had been trying to renew with John's grandfather for fourteen years was drawn up by Foscolo and signed in a matter of days on 2 June 1390. The treaty deals mainly with the familiar problems and grievances of the Venetian residents and traders in Constantinople. The national debt to Venice for damages still stood at 17,163 hyperpyra, which the Emperor John VII, in true imperial style, promised to pay in five annual instalments. He acknowledged that 30,000 ducats with interest had still to be found to redeem the Byzantine crown jewels, which John V had pawned to the Republic in partial fulfilment of his debts.[90]

Following his time in Constantinople Francesco Foscolo, together with Michele Contarini and Gabriele Emo, were elected joint Governors and military commanders of Argos (*Provveditore e Capitanîo di Argos*). [91] The Despot of Morea, Theodore I Palaiologos the youngest son of John V, with the aid of the Ottomans, had captured Nafplion and Argos in Morea (present day Peloponnese). The two cities had been sold to the Republic by its previous ruler, Maria of Enghien, following her Venetian husband's death in 1388.[92] These two cities were of strategic importance to the Republic, as they provided complete control of the shores of Morea. At the time of Francesco Foscolo's appointment, Nafplion had been retaken by the Republic, and efforts were now focused on the recovery of Argos. On Francesco's arrival he laid siege to the city. This siege would continue until 1394 when the city was recovered and formally ceded to the Republic.[93] Francesco Foscolo returned to Venice in 1392 and was elected to the prestigious post of Supervisor of monasteries.[94] He died in 1393 and was survived by his son Francesco.

15th – 16th Century

At the beginning of the 15th Century, following their victory against Genoa in the War of Chioggia, the Republic became the

---

[90] Nicol, D. M.: Byzantium and Venice: A study in cultural and deplomatic relations, Cambridge University Press, 1988, p.329
[91] Cicogna, E: Nelle Nozze Dell Nobile Daulo Augusto Di Foscolo Colla Baronessa Margh Degli Orefic, 1842 p. 10
[92] Luttrel, A: The Latins of Argos and Nauplia:1311 – 1394, Papers of the British School at Rome, 1966, p.34
[93] Nicol (n90)
[94] Senato Misti, Register 42, folio 199v copia

dominant naval power in the Adriatic and Aegean. It was a period of significant territorial expansion. By 1400 the Republic had enlarged its eastern trading bases, acquiring Corfu in the Ionian Islands, Nafplion and Argos in Morea (modern day Peloponnese), and Scutari and Durazzo in Albania. Territory in Dalmatia was acquired from King Ladislaus of Naples during the Hungarian civil war. He agreed to sell his rights to Dalmatian cities to the Republic for a meagre 100,000 ducats just before he lost his struggle and retreated to Naples. A truce with King Sigismund of Hungary in 1408 recognised the Republics' rights over this territory. The Republic used this to cease Trau, Spalato, Durazzo in 1420, consolidating their grip on Dalmatia (modern day Croatia). [95]

The Republic also made significant gains on the mainland following a War with Padua. This war came about after the Lord of Padua, Francesco II da Carrara, against the express wishes of the Republic, attempted to expand his territory following the death of The Duke of Milan, Galeazzo Visconti, in 1402. After an unsuccessful attempt to capture Brescia from Milan, the Lord of Padua turned his sights on capturing the Milanese cities of Verona and Vicenza, with the support from his son-in-law, Niccolò III d'Este, ruler of Ferrara, and Guglielmo della Scala, the heir to the Scaliger Lordship of Verona. [96] Verona was to be restored to the Scaliger, while Vicenza would come under Paduan rule. Verona was captured on 8 April 1404, and Guglielmo della Scala was acclaimed its Lord. With Verona secured, the Lord of

---

[95] Kiesewetter, A: LADISLAO d'Angiò Durazzo, re di Sicilia. Dizionario Enciclopedico degli Italiani, Enciclopedia Italiana, 2011
[96] Mallett, M: La conquista della Terraferma, Storia di Venezia dalle origini alla caduta della Serenissima, Vol. IV, Il'rinascimento: politica e cultura, Rome: Istituto della Enciclopedia Italiana. pp. 185-188

Padua focused on the siege of Vicenza. Rather than be captured, Vicenza chose to surrender itself to the protection of the Republic, and reluctantly the Lord of Padua withdrew his forces. In the meantime, in Verona, Guglielmo della Scala died on 15 April 1404, and the Lord of Padua deposed and arrested his two sons and claimed the lordship of Verona for himself.[97] Following this the Republic resolved to depose the Lord of Padua once and for all. A large Venetian force was mobilized against Padua and her ally Ferrara.[98] Venice quickly captured Belluno, Bassano, and Feltre. In October 1404 Verona was placed under siege. Rovigo was captured, and by late December 1404 troops were at the gates of Padua itself.[99] The threat posed by the Venetian fleet and troops to Ferrara forced Niccolò III d'Este to conclude a peace treaty with the Republic. The Lord of Padua's position then began to crumble.[100] On 26 May 1405, the strategic fortress at Castelcaro Basso fell to the Venetians.[101] On 22 June 1405, the citizens of Verona rose in revolt, forcing its governor, the Lord of Padua's son Jacopo, to accept the city's surrender to the Venetian forces. The surrender of Verona left the Venetians free to concentrate their forces against Padua, and after a lengthy siege, Padua fell on the 22nd of November 1405 ending the war.[102] The War resulted in the Republic expanding its territory on the mainland to cover most of Venetia, including the important cities

---

[97] Billanovich, G. & Chiara, M: Carara, Francesco da, il Novello, Dizionario Biografico degli Italiani, Vol 20: Carducci Carusi, Rome: Istituto dell Enciclopedia Italiana, 1977

[98] Mallett, M: La conquista della Terraferma, Storia di Venezia dalle origini alla caduta della Serenissima, Vol. IV, Il'rinascimento: politica e cultura, Rome: Istituto della Enciclopedia Italiana. pp. 184,185.

[99] Billanovich, (n97)

[100] Mallett (n98)

[101] Billanovich (n97)

[102] Mallett (n98), p. 188

of Padua, Verona, and Vicenza.

At this time, the Foscolo family lineage had descended to Nicolo and Andrea Foscolo, sons of Andrea, and their first cousin Francesco Foscolo, son of Francesco.

Nicolò Foscolo (1358-1425), son of Andrea, established himself as a powerful figure in the Senate. In 1395 he was elected to the Ducal Council[103]. At the time the Council was focused on matters related to Jewish lending in Venice. In 1338 the Republic had acquired a sizable Jewish community when it had annexed Mestre.[104] Financial difficulties caused by the Fourth Genovese War (1378 to 1381) had resulted in money lending being legalised in Venice, a practice which had been banned since 1254. All of those who participated in this business were Jews or associated with Jewish partners. To better accommodate the money lending business, in 1385 the Republic entered into an agreement (the Condotta) with money lending Jews in Mestre.[105] This permitted the Jews to undertake money lending activities in the City of Venice and allocated them land for use as a Jewish cemetery.[106] At this time Nicolo Foscolo was serving in the office for Jewish lending (*Cattaveri*), which was responsible for drafting the Candotta. [107] Until the Candotta there had been no Jewish community in Venice. On the signing of the Condotta many money lending Jews and their families began moving into the

---

[103] Maggior Consiglio, Register 21,Folio 82v
[104] Davis, R.C and Ravid, B: The Jews of Early Modern Venice, John Hopkins University Press, 2001, pp. 3-4
[105] Ibid p. 4
[106] Calimani, R., Sullam, A, and Calimani D.: The Venetian Ghetto, Mondadori, 2007 pp. 12, 90
[107] Segretario Voci Register 3, folio 7r

city.[108] This influx caused a great deal of concern in the local Christian community. Despite these tensions, the Condotta was extended in 1387 for a further 10 years, be it with an annual tax of 4,000 ducats imposed on Jews. Community tensions continued to rise until finally in 1394 the Ducal Council announced the Condotta would be allowed to lapse in 1397. A resolution was also proposed to expel all Jews from the City of Venice from that year. In 1395, it was Nicolò Foscolo together with his fellow Ducal Councillors Antonio Morosini and Marino Caravello that proposed a modified resolution. This allowed Jews not involved in money lending activities, such as doctors, to remain in the city. As black death was prevalent at the time Foscolo and his two fellow councillors no doubt believed the skills of Jewish doctors could be of great benefit to the city. Both resolutions were voted on by the Senate. However, animosity towards the Jews had reach such a level that the Senate voted 324 to 119 in favour of the earlier legislation, expelling all Jews from Venice.[109] Jews would not be allowed to live in the City of Venice again for another century[110].

In 1400, Nicolo Foscolo was elected to the Council of Forty, where in addition to hearing civil and criminal appeals, he was an elector of Doge Michele Steno.[111] In 1403, during the war with Padua, Nicolo Foscolo was appointed one of the three Chiefs of the Council of Ten,[112] and was again appointed a Chief of the

---

108 Calimani, R., Sullam, A, and Calimani D.: The Venetian Ghetto, Mondadori, 2007 pp. 12
109 Davis, R.C and Ravid, B: The Jews of Early Modern Venice, John Hopkins University Press, 2001, pp. 3-5
110 Ibid pp. 3-5
111 Maggior Consiglio Leona, Register 21, Folio 112r
112 Consiglio dei Dieci Misti, Register 8, Folio 87r

Council of Ten in 1405.[113] At the time of his second election, the Council of Ten was considering the fate of Francesco II da Carrara, the deposed Lord of Padua, his two sons, and a number of traitors within the Venetian Patriciate. After the surrender of Padua, Francesco II da Carrara, and his namesake son were brought to Venice. They were imprisoned in the Doge's Palace, where Jacopo, the second son of the Lord of Padua and former Governor of Verona was being held. The Republic normally pensioned off the ruling families of conquered cities. However, the da Carrara family were perceived as traitors, having been once allies of Venice and honoured with entry into the Venetian nobility. Furthermore, inquisition by the Council of Ten had uncovered plans to poison Venice's water supply, and there was considerable outrage as their captured account books showed that they had bribed Venetian nobles to serve as spies. The proposals ranged from imprisonment to exile in Candia (Crete) or Cyprus.[114] In the end, Nicolò Foscolo together with other members of the Council of Ten went one step further. They concluded the members of the da Carrara family were too dangerous to be left alive and decree they be put to death. Francesco II da Carrara was strangled on the 17th of January 1406, and his two sons followed a few days later. This harsh sentence was welcomed by the Venetian populace, with news of the execution provoking no sympathies other than the phrase "dead men wage no wars".[115]

In 1408 Nicolò Foscolo was elected the Governor of Modon

---

[113] Consiglio dei Dieci – Misti Register 8, Folio 148r
[114] Billanovich, G. & Chiara, M: Carara, Francesco da, il Novello, Dizionario Biografico degli Italiani, Vol 20: Carducci Carusi, Rome: Istituto dell Enciclopedia Italiana, 1977
[115] Lane, F: Venice, a maritime republic, Johns Hopkins University Press, 1973 pp. 227-228

(*Rettore Castellano di Modone*), Morea (modern day Peloponnese) [116] where he was part of a military campaign attempting to increase the Republics power and influence in Morea. Theodore I Palaiologos, the Despot of Morea, had died in the previous year and there was a period of instability in the region prior to the succession. [117] The Republic had taken the opportunity to take Lapanto in 1407, and in 1408 ceased Patra and the land around it. The strongholds of Lepanto and Patra were strategically important to the Republic. Amongst other things, they helped keep check on Ottoman pirates, which were making the Gulf of Corinth unsafe for merchant shipping at the time.[118] It was Nicolò Foscolo who wrote to the Ducal Council from Modon to report that Fantino Michele, commander of the naval fleet in the Adriatic (*Capitanîo Golfo*), had with forty crossbow troops successfully taken the fortress of Patra held by the Duke of Morea, and had removed 1500 ducats found in the Castle of Lepanto for fear it would fall into the hands of Ottoman pirates.[119]

Nicolò Foscolo was responsible for much of the early construction of the fortifications at Modon. The Foscolo family coat of arms adorns the lower sea gate of the castle to this day. It can also be found together with the coat of arms of the Bembo and Foscarini families on the Bembo bastion, an impressive quadrilateral bastion designed to protect the northwest angle of the castle from

---

116 Sanuto, R. I. S. tom xxii, p. 837
117 Nicol, M.D: The Last Centuries of Byzantium, 1261-1453, Cambridge: Cambridge University Press, 1993
118 Brill, E.J: First Encyclopaedia of Islam: 1913-1936, Vol 3, Leiden, New York, 1993 p.571
119 Cicogna, E: Nelle Nozze Dell Nobile Daulo Augusto Di Foscolo Colla Baronessa Margh Degli Orefic,1842, Sanuto, R. I. S. tom xxii p. 837

artillery bombardment.

After his term on Modon Nicolò Foscolo was appointed as commander of the naval fleet in the Adriatic (*Capitanîo Golfo*). His appointment came about after several patricians refused election to the post. Commanding ten armed galleys, his time in the post was largely uneventful.[120] Shortly after his return to Venice in 1414, Nicolò Foscolo was elected to the Council of Forty, and was an elector of Doge Tommaso Mocenigo.[121]

In 1417 he was elected to the prestigious post of Governor of Corfu (*Bailo Corfu*).[122] On his return to Venice in 1423, Nicolò Foscolo was elected to the Council of Forty and was an elector of the famous and unhappy Doge Francesco Foscari.[123] Nicolò Foscolo died around 1425 and was succeeded by his son Andrea.

At the same time as the afore mentioned Nicolò Foscolo, lived his brother, **Andrea Foscolo (1363-1438)**, son of Andrea. In 1399 he was elected Governor of Drivasto an outpost in Albania (*Podestà di Drivasto*).[124] A few years later, in 1416, Andrea Foscolo together with Delfino Venier were elected joint Administrators of the Venetian Navy.[125] Their appointment came at a critical time. A few years earlier, in 1413, the Ottoman civil war had ended, and Mehmed I had proclaimed himself Sultan.[126]

---

[120] Sanuto, R. I. S. tom xxii, ibid, p. 840
[121] Maggior Consiglio, Leona, Register 21, folio 230v, 1414
[122] AvC, Raspe, Record, 3647, Folio 87r, 1417
[123] Cicogna, E: Nelle Nozze Dell Nobile Daulo Augusto Di Foscolo Colla Baronessa Margh Degli Orefic, 1842, p. 11
[124] Senato Misti, Register 44, folio 128v, 1399
[125] Sanudo, Tom XXII pp. 899–90
[126] Lewis, B, Pellat, C. & Schacht, J: The Encyclopaedia of Islam, New Edition, Volume II, 1965 p. 975

Citadel at Modone, Camocio Giovanni Francesco 1574

Remains of the fortifications at Mordon

Foscolo blazon right at the first sea gate Modon

Foscolo blazon right, carved into the foundation stone of Bembo Bastion at Modon

The Republic was eager to renew treaties it had concluded with Mehmed's predecessors. However, this had been frustrated by the inability of the Republic's Ambassador to Constantinople to meet with the Sultan. Mehmed I had been involved with a military campaign in Anatolia, and it was Venetian policy at the time for the Ambassador not to leave Constantinople. Mehmed I became frustrated at the delay.[127] In addition, the Lord of Andros, as well as the Duke of Naxos, both Venetian citizens and vassals of the Republic, had been conducting raids against Ottoman shipping.[128] In retaliation, in 1414, the Ottoman fleet ravaged the islands of Andros, Paros, and Milos, carrying off a large part of the inhabitants to be sold as slaves.[129] In the same year, the Ottomans raided the Venetian colony of Euboea (modern day Evia, Greece) and pillaged its capital, Negroponte, taking its 2,000 in habitants as slaves.[130] The Following year, In 1415, the Ottoman fleet attempted to intercept a Venetian merchant convoy coming from the Black Sea at the island of Tenedos. The convoy managed to outrun the Ottoman fleet.[131] However, the Ottomans attacked the fortress of Oreos (Loreo in northern Evia), and once again ravage the island. [132] These actions by the Ottomans challenged Venetian naval hegemony in the Aegean. It also spread considerable panic amongst its colonists, and impacted trade with the east as it became prohibitively expensive

---

[127] Fabris, A:From Adrianople to Constantinople: Venetian–Ottoman diplomatic missions, 1360–1453, Mediterranean Historical Review, 7 (2), 1992 pp. 172, 173

[128] Sanudo, Tom XXII pp. 899–90

[129] Miller, W: The Latins in the Levant: A History of Frankish Greece (1204–1566), John Murray, London, 1908 pp. 598–59

[130] Fabris (n127), p. 174

[131] Sanudo (n128)

[132] Manfroni, C: La battaglia di Gallipoli e la politica veneto-turca (1381-1420), L'Ateneo Veneto, Venice. XXV (II), 1902 p. 137

to crew merchant ships heading to the north Aegean.[133] In 1416, Andrea Foscolo and Delfino Venier arranged armed escorts for merchant ships, to ensure the Republics all important trade routes were not undermined, and to some extent restore public confidence.[134]

Later in 1416 Andrea Foscolo and Delfino Venier were dispatched to the Dardanelles as emissaries of the Republic to meet with the Ottoman Sultan. Pietro Loredan was named Commander of the Adriatic Fleet (*Capitanîo Golfo*). He was ordered by the Senate to convey Andrea Foscolo and Delfino Venier to the Dardanelles, and in the event their negotiations with the Sultan failed, he was instructed to launch an attack on the Ottomans.[135] Foscolo and Venier were named joint administrators of the fleet (*Provveditore d'Armata*), which flew the standard of Saint Marco.[136] On their arrival the Venetian fleet was attacked by the Ottomans. This naval action became known as the battle of Gallipoli. The Venetian fleet, in a seven-hour confrontation, defeated the Ottoman fleet capturing twenty-seven vessels. Four thousand Ottomans perished and one thousand one hundred Christians in the paid service of the Ottomans were taken as slaves. Venetian casualties were light with twelve dead and three hundred injured. Fortunately, one of the Ottoman Captains taken prisoner composed a letter to the Sultan, stating that the Venetians had been attacked without cause. The negotiations went ahead. Dolfino Venier was tasked with negotiating a peace

---

[133] Fabris, A: From Adrianople to Constantinople: Venetian–Ottoman diplomatic missions, 1360–1453, Mediterranean Historical Review, 7 (2), 1992, pp. 172, 173
[134] Manfroni, C: La battaglia di Gallipoli e la politica veneto-turca (1381-1420), L'Ateneo Veneto, Venice. XXV (II), 1902, p. 139
[135] Manfroni, (n134), p. 141
[136] Sanudo, Tom XXII pp. 899–90

agreement with the Sultan, and as part of those negotiations, Andrea Foscolo led a mission to the Principality of Achaea (Peloponnese peninsular), at the time a Latin-Christian vassal state of the Republic.[137] Dolfino Venier reached an agreement with the Sultan, but on his return to Venice it was not well received and later declared void. The agreement had to be renegotiated with Mehmed's successor, Sultan Murad I in 1430, and Dolfino Venier found himself under trial by the Council of Ten.[138] For his part, Andrea Foscolo had been successful.

In 1423, Andrea Foscolo was elected military commander of Vicenza (*Capitanîo di Vicenza*). His appointment came just before the Lombardy wars of 1423 to 1454, when the Duchy of Milan began to encroach on Venetian territory in northern Italy. In Vicenza Andrea Foscolo was tasked with strengthening the defences of the city in the lead up to the war.[139] The Republic did not enter the first campaign of the war until 1425 when they signed a pact with Florence against Milan. They lay siege to Breccia which fell to the Republic. In 1426 the Republic gained Breccia as part of the peace settlement at the end of the first campaign. However, the peace did not last long with Milan refusing to ratify the peace settlement, and hostilities broke out again in 1427. The second campaign of the war ended in 1429 with the Republic gaining Bergamo and Crema.[140]

A few years later Andrea Foscolo had returned to the Senate, when in 1428, news of a debt crisis on Candia (modern day Crete) reached Venice. Debtors petitioned the Senate to cancel their

---

137 Sanudo, Tom XXII p. 146
138 Ibid pp. 174-175
139 Cappellari, Reggimenti, Il mss
140 Arrighi, G: The Long Twentieth Century, Verso, 1994

debts to Jewish lenders, who they complained had lent money on unjust terms.[141] Unlike some states in Latin Christendom at the time, Venice did not cancel the debt, as they saw Jewish lending as a vital part of the economy and wanted it to continue. However, after hearing from representatives of both the Jewish and Latin communities on Candia, the Senate ordered a commission of three noblemen to work out compromise settlements. Ironically, not one Candian nobleman could be found who did not owe a debt to the Jews. For this reason, three Venetian Patricians were sent to deal with the crisis. Andrea Foscolo, together with Marco Zeno Cavaliere, and Zaccaria Valaresso, were dispatched as joint Governors of Candia (*Provveditore di Candia*). Their task, among other things, was to hold a commission to impose more just terms on debtors, especially Venetian Patricians.[142] The commission succeeded in accomplishing the delicate task to the satisfaction of all parties. The interest rate on the debts being reduced from 10% to 5%.[143] A few years after his return to Venice, in 1438, Andrea Foscolo died. He was succeeded by his sons Girolamo and Paolo Foscolo.

The first cousin of the afore mentioned brothers Andrea and Nicolò Foscolo, also lived in the early part of the 15th Century. **Francesco Foscolo (1350-1428)**, son of Francesco, spent most of his career in the Senate, and in 1423, was elected one of the first Governors of Friuli (*Luogotenente della Patria del Friuli*).[144] At the time of Francesco Foscolo's election the Patria del Friuli had been gained by the Republic a few years earlier. The

---

141 Corano, A: Storia di Candia, Creta Sacra ii, MSS, pp. 381,382
142 ibid
143 Rena, L: Venice's Colonial Jews: Community, Identity, and Justice in Late Medieval Venetian Crete. Thesis, Harvard, 2014
144 Palladio, Storia del Friuli, II, Miss, p. 13

territory had been under the rule of the Patriarch of Aquileia, and one of the ecclesiastical states of the Holy Roman Empire. In around 1400, the Patriarchate of Aquileia suffered internal conflict between the cities of Cividale and Udine. In 1411 this escalated into a civil war. Cividale received support from most of the Friulian communes and King Sigismund of Hungary, while Udine was backed by the Republic. In December 1411 King Sigismund's army captured Udine, and Louis of Teck was installed as patriarch in the city's cathedral. However, on 23 July 1419 the Republic conquered Cividale and laid siege to Udine, which fell on 7 June 1420. Soon afterwards Gemona, San Daniele, Venzone and Tolmezzo fell to the Republic. On 7 July 1420 the former Friulian state became a territory of the Venetian Republic and was named Patria del Friuli. It was ruled by a Venetian Governor (*Luogotenente*) living in Udine. Friuli maintained some form of autonomy, by keeping its own Parliament on the old territory of the Patriarchate, an autonomy not granted to other cities and provinces under the control of the Republic. The rest of the territory of Patria del Friuli maintained the old nobility, which was able to keep their feudal rights over the land and its inhabitants.[145] It was not until 1445 that the war officially ended, after Doge Francesco Foscari signed an agreement with King Sigismund of Hungary in 1433, and after the Patriarch Ludovico Trevisan at the Council of Florence acquiesced to the loss of his ancient temporal estate in 1445.[146] At the time Francesco Foscolo took up his appointment, in 1423, the situation in the Patria del Friuli had normalised, and his time in office was dominated by transitional issues, such as taxation and various issues

---

[145] Shahan, T: Aquileia, in Catholic Encyclopidia, Vol 1 Robert Appleton, New York, 1907

[146] ibid

surrounding the operation of feudal rights. Francesco Foscolo died without heirs around 1428.[147]

In the mid 15th Century, the Foscolo family lineage progressed to Andrea Foscolo, son of Nicolò, and his first cousins, Girolamo and Paolo Foscolo, sons of Andrea.

Andrea Foscolo (1386 - 1458), son of Nicolò, served in the Senate between 1439 to 1444.[148] Early in 1444 he was elected Ambassador to Constantinople (*Bailo di Costantinopoli*), a highly sort after and prestigious post.[149] Leading up to Andrea's term as Ambassador, Emperor John VIII of Constantinople had in 1442 signed an agreement extending for a further five years the privileges of the Venetian colony in his city, and in 1443 the Pope had announced a crusade in defence of the eastern Christians against the Ottomans. The Crusade of Varna was the last attempt by western Christendom to drive the Ottomans out of Europe. The Republic had committed to the crusade, for a price, eight armed galleys under the command of Alvise Loredan. The fleet was under the command of Cardinal Francesco Condulmer and its ships flew the Pope's standard. Around the time Andrea Foscolo arrived in Constantinople, the crusade had founded, mainly because of poor organisation, division of purpose and lack of co-ordination. In 1445 Emperor John VIII sent an ambassador to Venice to announce that he was appealing to Charles VII of France, Philip of Burgundy, and the Pope, for further assistance in the crusade. Cardinal Condulmer stayed in Constantinople with a few ships in the belief that the Hungarians were planning

---

[147] Palladio, Storia del Friuli, II, Miss, p. 13
[148] Segretario Voci Register 4, folio 100r, 1439, folio 103r, 1340, folio 105v, 1341, folio 105v, 1342, folio 108v, 1342 folio 111r, 1343
[149] Segretario Voci Register 4, folio 86v, 1344

to resurrect the Crusade at any time. The Venetians were rightly sceptical on this point. They could not wait for miracles. Towards the end of 1445 Andrea Foscolo was directed by the Senate to negotiate peace with the Ottomans. Alvise Loredan was ordered to stay in the straits with the Papal Legate until peace was concluded. He was to consult with Andrea Foscolo on an agreement that ensured freedom for Venetian merchants in the Sultan's dominions. The agreement took the form of an earlier treaty signed with the Ottoman Sultan in 1430, which coincidently Andrea's grandfather, Andrea Foscolo (1363-1438), had played a part in negotiating. After the battle at Varna, Sultan Murad had unexpectedly opted to retire and to hand over to his son Mehmed II. It was a strange and premature decision. Murad was no more than forty years old. His son was not yet thirteen. To be on the safe side, Andrea Foscolo and Alvise Loredan thought it wise to make peace with both. Despite the Pope's displeasure, Andrea Foscolo met with Murad in Edirne, where he was received with great honour. The elder Sultan took Foscolo in his confidence and spoke at length, including on personal matters such as his view on old age. A treaty was agreed. The young Sultan Mehmed II signed the agreement on 23 February 1446.[150]

On his return from Constantinople, Andrea Foscolo was elected in March 1447 to the Council of Ten.[151] At the time the council was occupied with matters closer to home. The Lombardy wars, which had commenced in 1423, were ongoing. The Third Campaign (1431-1433) and Fourth campaign (1438-1441) had resulted in a virtual stalemate, with the Republic gaining Ravenna in 1441.[152] During the fourth campaign Francesco Sforza, a well-regarded

---

[150] Woodhead, C.: The Ottoman World, Routledge Press, 2012 p.138
[151] Segretario Voci Register 4, folio 117r, 1447
[152] Arrighi, G: The Long Twentieth Century, Verso, 1994

mercenary, had fought valiantly for the Republic, and several Patricians formed close links with the Sforza family. However, their connection with the family became a dangerous and suspect one, when Francesco Sforza deserted Venice in 1447 following his marriage to the daughter of the Duke of Milan. The Council of Ten launched an investigation into the matter. It revealed that several Patricians including the Doge's only surviving son, Jacopo Foscari, and possibly even the Doge himself, had been rather too friendly with Sforza and had received money from him. The Doge's son-in-law, Andrea Donato, was accused of receiving a bribe of 100 ducats from Sforza. He was recalled from his post as Doge of Candia and tried by the Council of Ten. He was found guilty and sent into exile. The Doge's son, Jacopo Foscari, was also tried by the Council of Ten and exiled to Nafplio. This sentence was commuted to exile to Zelarino, a town in Treviso over which the Foscari family held feudal rights. However, in September 1447, Andrea Foscolo together with the other members of the Council of Ten, issued Jacopo Foscari a full pardon.[153]

In 1448 Andrea Foscolo returned to the Senate, where he served until 1450.[154] Then in 1451 he was again elected to the Council of Ten.[155] At this time the Council was once again occupied with a delicate case involving the Doge's only son, Jacopo Foscari. In November 1450, Ermolao Donà, who had attracted much hatred during his term as public prosecutor (*Avogadoria de Comùn*) was murdered. An investigation into the murder was immediately undertaken by the Council of Ten. It was January 1451 when the

---

[153] Von Bode, W: Eine Porträtplakette des Dogen Francesco Foscari von Donatello: Ein Nachtrag, Berliner Museen 45 (2), . 1924, Pp. 42–430.
[154] Segretario Voci Register 4, folio 128v, 1450
[155] Segretario Voci Register 4, folio 130r, 1451

Council of Ten ordered the arrest of Foscari on information provided by Antonio Venier, who himself was known as being of questionable character. For three months Andrea Foscolo and other members of the Council tried to convince themselves of Foscari's guilt. Several attempts were made to get the accused to confess under torture. In the absence of conclusive evidence, and lacking a confession, Andrea Foscolo and other members of the Council were unable to pass sentence. Finally, they resolved to send Foscari into perpetual exile in Chania (Modern day Crete).[156]

Following his term on the Council of Ten, Andrea Foscolo was in 1452 elected administrator of wheat and grain supplies in Venice (*Provveditore alle Biade*).[157] This was a special appointment that came about following a poor harvest on the mainland, which undermined food security in the Republic. Andrea Foscolo was responsible for the critical task of securing, and where necessary, rationing food supplies.

In 1453, Andrea Foscolo was elected to the powerful Ducal Council.[158] In the year of his election Constantinople fell to the Ottomans. Andrea Foscolo in the Signoria (consisting of the Ducal Council and three Chiefs of the Council of Forty) argued strongly in favour of pursuing a peace settlement with Sultan Mehmed II, to retain trading privileges in Constantinople. The policy was adopted by the Signoria, and an agreement was ratified by the Sultan in 1454, with the all-important trading concessions restored.[159] At the same time on the mainland, following four

---

[156] Von Bode, W: Eine Porträtplakette des Dogen Francesco Foscari von Donatello: Ein Nachtrag, Berliner Museen 45 (2), . 1924, Pp. 42–430

[157] Segretario Voci Register 4, folio 134r, 1452

[158] Segretario Voci Register 4, folio 94r, 1453

[159] Nichol, D. M.: Byzantium and Venice: A study in cultural and deplomatic relations, Cambridge University Press, 1988

military campaign and no decisive result, Andrea Foscolo and other members of the Ducal Council were heavily engaged in negotiations with Milan to end the Lombardy wars. The peace was to be mediated by Francesco Sforza, who was confirmed as the rightful Duke of Milan. These negotiations were of great importance to the Republic and resulted in the Treaty of Lodi being signed in 1454, where territorial boundaries were agreed along the river Adda between the Milanese and Venetians. Brescia and Bergamo were reconfirmed as gains by the Republic. The treaty of Lodi gave rise to the five mainland powers of the 15th Century, namely Venice, Milan, Florence, the Papal States, and Naples. The balance between these powers resulted in a period of relative peace lasting 40 years, until French intervention resulted in War in 1494.[160] A year later in 1454 Andrea Foscolo was elected one of the three wise men of the chambers of the mainland domains *(Provveditore sopra Camere)*, a senior magistracy responsible for tax collection.[161]

In June 1456, the Doge's Son Jacopo Foscari was once again accused. On this occasion he was said to have entered correspondence with Francesco Sforza, and even with Sultan Mehmed II, in a plot to form an alliance against the Republic. Foscari was brought back to Venice from his exile in Crete and tried by the Council of Ten. Even though there were grave misgivings regarding his guilt, he confessed without the application of torture. The Council of Ten imposed the lightest punishment possible, merely confirming his exile to Crete. The Doge and the young man's family were given permission to visit-

---

[160] Mattingly, G: Renaissance Diplomacy, Cosimo Classics, published 2010 p.178
[161] Segretario Voci Register 4, folio 30r, 1454

Foscolo Family of Venice: Patricans and Aristocrats (A Genealogy)

Map Showing boarders after the treaty of Lodi 1454

him in prison prior to his exile. Jacopo pleaded with his father for a pardon. However, so as not to undermine his own position as Doge, it was refused, and Jacopo was told to accept his punishment. About a week after his return to Crete Jacopo Foscari died. This provoked such public outcry in Venice that he was given a state funeral. A year later Francesco Foscari, wracked with grief and guilt following the death of his only son became withdrawn and unable to perform his duties. The Council of Ten forced him to abdicate.[162] It was shortly after this, in 1457, Andrea Foscolo was elected to the Council of Forty and was an elector of Doge Pasquale Malipiero.[163] Andrea Foscolo died around 1458 and was survived by his son Marco.

The first cousin of the afore mentioned Andrea Foscolo, **Girolamo Foscolo (1401-1465)**, son of Andrea, was a well-respected Senator. In 1441 he was elected to the Council of Forty, judging civil and criminal appeals,[164] and following this he was elected the military commander of Rovereto (*Capitanîo di Rovereto*).[165] In 1443, Girolamo Foscolo was elected Governor and military commander of Mestre (*Podestà e Capitanîo di Mestre*).[166] Then in 1444 he became the Supreme Consul of the Merchants (*sopra consoli dei Mercanti*), a senior magistrate responsible for judging bankruptcy petitions. [167] In 1447, Girolamo Foscolo was elected administrator of gold coinage (*Massari alla moneta d'oro*).[168] A few years later, in 1453, he was

---

162 Von Bode, W: Eine Porträtplakette des Dogen Francesco Foscari von Donatello: Ein Nachtrag, Berliner Museen 45 (2), 1924, Pp. 42–430.
163 Maggior Consiglio, Register 23, folio 16v, 1457
164 Segretario Voci Register 4, folio 103vr, 1441
165 Segretario Voci Register 4, folio 61r, 1441
166 Segretario Voci Register 4, folio 53r, 1443
167 Segretario Voci Register 4, folio 30v, 1444
168 Segretario Voci Register 4, folio 19v, 1447

elected military commander of Serravalle (*Capitanîo di Serravalle*).[169] In the following year, 1454, Girolamo Foscolo travelled in an official capacity through mainland states as a senior magistrate (*auditori nuovi*),[170] hearing appeals from the Republic's subjects, inspecting the exercise of justice, and where necessary investigating the conduct of resident officials. In 1458, he was elected Governor of Murano (*Podestà di Murano*), at the time an important commercial centre and home to the Republics critical glass production facilities.[171] Then in 1460, he was elected Governor of Lepanto in the Gulf of Corinth (*Rettore di Lepanto*).[172] His time in the post was largely uneventful. He returned to Venice where he took up his position in the Senate before his death in around 1465. He was succeeded by his sons Nicolo, Andrea, Pietro, and Alvise.

The brother of the afore mentioned Girolamo Foscolo, **Paolo Foscolo (1396-1452)** son of Andrea, entered the Great Council in 1429, and was elected Consul to Tunisia in 1439 (*Console di Tunisi*).[173] Shortly after his return to Venice, in 1440, he was elected Governor of Pirano, Istria (*Podestà di Pirano*).[174] A few years later, in 1444, he was elected a senior magistrate responsible for judging non-fatal brawls between commoners (*Cinque alla Pace*).[175] In 1445, Paolo Foscolo travelled through the mainland states as one of three senior magistrates (*auditori*

---

169 Segretario Voci Register 4, folio 55r, 1453
170 Segretario Voci Register 4, folio 54r, 1454
171 Segretario Voci Register 5, folio 7v, 1458
172 Hope, C: Chroniques Greco-Romanes, Avec Notes et Tables Genealogiques, Berlin, 1873, p. 391
173 Segretario Voci Register 4, folio 85r, 1439
174 Segretario Voci Register 5, folio 11v, 1440
175 Segretario Voci Register 4, folio 37V, 1444

nuovi).[176] He returned to Venice in 1447 and later that year was elected one of the senior magistrates responsible for public accounting (*Ufficiali alle Rason Vecchie*).[177] He returned to the Senate in 1449[178] before being elected in 1450 Ambassador to Trebisonda (*Bailo di Trebisonda*).[179] At the time Trebisonda was an important Venetian trading hub on the black sea, and the role of Ambassador was a sort after position. Paolo Foscolo died in around 1452 and was succeeded by his son Andrea Foscolo.

In the mid 15th Century early 16th Century, the Foscolo family lineage progressed to Marco Foscolo, son of Andrea, and his first cousins Nicolo, Alvise, Andrea, Pietro Foscolo, sons of Girolamo, and Andrea Foscolo son of Paolo. The historical records make little mention of Nicolo or Alvise sons of Girolamo, who entered the Great Council but did not hold any military or civil posts of note.

Marco Foscolo (1422-1506), son of Andrea, had a notable career in the Senate. He entered the Great Council in 1442 and spent his early years serving in the internal Magistracy's. In 1447 he was elected Governor of Este (*Podestà di Este*).[180] A few years after his return to Venice in 1450, Marco Foscolo spent two years as an officer at the ternary (*Ufficiali alla Ternaria Vecchia*).[181] The office responsible for controlling trade imports. In this role he was responsible for collecting import duties and arrears and issuing warrants for the unloading of goods. Then in 1453 he was elected to the Council of Forty, where he judged civil and criminal

---

176 Segretario Voci Register 4, folio 154r, 1445
177 Segretario Voci Register 4, folio 27r, 1447
178 Segretario Voci Register 4, folio 122v, 1449
179 Segretario Voci Register 4, folio 86r, 1450
180 Segretario Voci Register 4, folio 58v, 1447
181 Segretario Voci Register 4, folio 43v, 1450

appeals.[182] He returned to the internal Magistracy's, where in 1471 he was elected as one of the senior magistrates responsible for public accounting (*Ufficiali alle Rason Nuove*).[183] In 1474 Marco Foscolo was elected to the Council of Forty, where he was an elector of Doge Pietro Mocenigo.[184] Mocenigo's term as Doge did not last long. He died two years after his election of malaria.[185] In 1476 Marco Foscolo was once again elected to the Council of Forty and was an elector of Doge Andrea Vendramin.[186] This was a famously controversial election, with the Council of Forty far from unanimous in its decision. Marco Foscolo himself was in the camp opposed to the election of Vendramin. The election caused much animosity within the patriciate, with Antonio Feleto imprisoned and banished in 1477 for remarking in public that the Council of Forty must have been hard pressed to elect a cheesemonger Doge.[187,188] Andrea Vendramins' term as Doge was short, as he fell victim to the black death in 1478.[189] Marco Foscolo was again elected to the Council of Forty in 1478 where he was an elector of Doge Giovanni Mocenigo.[190]

In late 1478 Marco Foscolo was appointed a Senior Magistrate (*Savi in Rialto*).[191] In this post he was responsible for preparing

---

182 Segretario Voci Register 4, folio 135v, 1453
183 Segretario Voci Register 6, folio 39v, 1471
184 Maggior Consiglio, Register 23, folio 145v, 1474
185 Lane, Frederic C :Family Partnerships and Joint Ventures in the Venetian Republic, Journal of Economic History. 4 (2), 1944) p. 179
186 Maggior Consiglio, Register 23, folio 157v, 1476
187 Malipiero, D:. Annali veneti dall'anno 1457 al 1500, Editors, Francesco Longo (Senatore.), Agostino Sagredo, Vieusseux, 1843
188 Coriolano, C & Kiril, P: The Deeds of Commander Pietro Mocenigo in Three Books, Italic Press, 2014
189 ibid
190 Maggior Consiglio, Register 23, folio 177v, 1478
191 Segretario Voci Register 6, folio 109r, 1483

the government's agenda, drafting legislation, and supervising its execution. In 1484, Marco Foscolo was elected to the Ducal Council. At the time of his appointment the Council was engaged in peace negotiations following a war with Ferrarra. In 1482 Venice had allied with Pope Sixtus IV in his attempt to conquer Ferrara. Ferrara was allied with Florence, Naples, Milan, and Ercole d'Este. When Papal-Venetian forces were defeated at the Battle of Campomorto, Pope Sixtus IV changed sides. Left to fight alone, the Venetians were defeated. The balance was changed yet again by Ludovico Sforza of Milan, who ultimately sided with Venice. This shift in power led to peace negotiations. The terms of the peace treaty were agreed by the Signoria, which included Marco Foscolo and other members of the Ducal Council, together with the three Chiefs of the Council of Forty. The treaty was signed near Brescia on 7 August 1484.[192]

In 1485 Marco Foscolo returned to the Council of Forty, after the poisoning of Doge Giovanni Mocenigo[193], and was an elector of Doge Marco Barbarigo.[194] When Barbarigo died shortly after his election in a dispute with other nobles in 1486[195], Marco Foscolo again found himself on the Council of Forty, and was an elector of his brother Doge Agostino Barbarigo.[196,197] Marco Foscolo was then elected multiple times to both the Council of Ten (1493,

---

192 Tuohy, T: Herculean Ferrara: Ercole d'este, 1471-1505, and the intervention of a Ducal Capital, Cambridge University Press, 1996
193 Malipiero, D:. Annali veneti dall'anno 1457 al 1500, Editors, Francesco Longo (Senatore.), Agostino Sagredo, Vieusseux, 1843
194 Maggior Consiglio, Register 24, folio 62r, 1485
195 Malipiero (n193)
196 Maggior Consiglio, Register 24, folio 76r, 1486
197 Malipiero (n193)

1495)[198,199,] and to the Ducal Council (1491 and 1499).[200,201] In 1502 he was again elected to the Council of Forty and was an elector of Doge Leonardo Loredan.[202] He was again elected to the Ducal Council in 1503,[203] which at the time was occupied with the peace treaty to conclude the Second Ottoman Venetian War, when Venetians conceded significant territory to the Ottomans. Marco Foscolo died in 1504, and was succeeded by his sons Andrea and Zacaria, to whom he left a large inheritance of 25,000 ducats.[204]

16th - 17th Century

Venice entered the 16th Century at the peak of its power, both in terms of its foreign and mainland territories, and it's financial and military strength. Having enjoyed a relatively peaceful period at the end of the 15th Century, what followed was a century of war. The 16th Century culminated in the Republic losing its territorial possessions, its trading monopolies, and its financial and military strength. Its troubles stemmed from two further Italian wars on the mainland, and conflicts with an increasingly emboldened Ottoman Empire.

A member of the Foscolo family involved in the Italian Wars, and heavily involved in the military campaign against the Ottomans, was **Andrea Foscolo (1450-1528)**, second son of Girolamo and Chiara Garzoni. Andrea joined the Great Council at a young

---

198 Segretario Voci Register 9, folio 3v, 1493
199 Segretario Voci Register 9, folio 8r, 1495
200 Segretario Voci Register 7, folio 0r, 1491
201 Segretario Voci Register 7, folio 1r , 1499
202 Maggior Consiglio, Register 24, folio 187r, 1501
203 Segretario Voci Register 7, folio 1v , 1503
204 Sanudo VI, 25

age in 1471, and by 1489 he was one of the three Chiefs of the Council of Forty. Later in 1490, Andrea became Judge of Petitions hearing bankruptcy appeals from the Consul of the Merchants. In 1496, Andrea was elected Governor of Orzinuovi (*lieutenant Orzinuovi*).[205] This turned out to be a delicate and important position. In 1498, Louis XII of France had claimed the Duchy of Milan by right of his paternal grandmother Valentina Visconti. This led to the Second Italian War. Louis XII entered an alliance with the Republic, against the Dutchy of Milan. In 1499 preparations got underway to attack Milan at Cremona and Ghiara d'Adda.[206] At nearby Orzinuovi, Andrea distinguished himself by organizing troops in readiness for the attack. He also worked on strengthening the defensive apparatus of the fortress.[207] The campaign was ultimately successful, the Republic gained Cremona, and Louis XII made his triumphant entrance into Milan in October 1499 declaring himself Duke of Milan[208].

On his return to Venice in 1499, Andrea Foscolo was elected the naval commander from Venice through the entire Western Mediterranean to the Spanish coastal port of Aigues-Mortes (*Capitanîo di Muda Aigues-Mortes*).[209] However, in the same year the Ottoman sultan attacked the Venetian fortress at Lepanto by land and sent a large fleet to support the offensive by sea. The Venetian fleet under the command of Antonio Grimani was defeated in 1499 by the Ottomans in the sea battle of Zonchio

---

[205] Gullino, G; Andrea Foscolo, Dizionario Biografico degli Italiani, Vol 49, 1997
[206] Guérard, A: France: A Modern History, University of Michigan, 1959 p.128
[207] Cicogna, E: Nelle Nozze Dell Nobile Daulo Augusto Di Foscolo Colla Baronessa Margh Degli Orefic, 1842, p. 12
[208] Guérard (n206) p. 128
[209] Gullino (n205)

(modern day Pylos, Greece), and Lepanto was lost. It was the beginning of the Second Venetian-Ottoman war 1499 to 1503. Andrea deployed eastward to attack Kefalonia, which had fallen to the Ottomans, but the fortress proved impregnable.[210] He was then appointed Vice-Captain of Large Galleys, and with these he participated in the attack of the Ottoman held Island of Tenedos (an island of Turkey in the north-eastern part of the Aegean Sea). Following this, he again attacked Kefalonia, on this occasion together with the Spanish fleet led by Gonzalo de Cordoba. The attack succeeded and the island fell into Venetian hands in 1501. This was a significant victory, as it stopped the Ottoman offensive on the eastern Venetian territories.[211] Shortly after this victory, Andrea was elected Deputy Administrator of the Venetian Army, and participated in the campaign of Zonchio (the second battle of Lapanto) which the Venetian's lost to the Ottomans.[212]

In 1503, with no appetite for all-out war with the Ottomans, the Republic surrendered their base at Lepanto, Durazzo, Modon and Coron, to the Ottomans.[213] The peace treaty was negotiated by the Signoria, which included Andrea's first cousin Marco Foscolo (1422-1504).

Shortly after his military campaigns, Andrea Foscolo entered civil administration. He balloted several times between 1503 and 1506 to become Ambassador to Constantinople (*Bailo Constantinopli*) but failed each time. He was instead elected a senior magistrate. Andrea had not yet reached the end of his mandate in the

---

210 Cicogna, E: Nelle Nozze Dell Nobile Daulo Augusto Di Foscolo Colla Baronessa Margh Degli Orefic, 1842, p. 12
211 Gullino, G; Andrea Foscolo, Dizionario Biografico degli Italiani, Vol 49, 1997
212 Sanuto, Nei Diarii mss, nella marciana, vol III
213 ibid

magistracies, when in 1507 he finally managed to secure election to the lucrative post of Ambassador to Constantinople. At the time Venetian-Ottoman relations were completely calm, as Sultan Bayazid II was engaged in a campaign against the Persians in the east. The only aftermath of the 1499 to 1503 war was the release of prisoners. [214] The Ottomans had made it known to Andrea that if he did not bring 15,000 ducats with him to secure their release, the unfortunates would be sawed in half whilst alive as required by Islamic custom. Andrea arrived in the Bosporus in April 1508, secured the release of all prisoners, and witness the conclusion of the peace between Persia and the Sultan Bayazid-II.[215]

Sometime into Andreas term as Ambassador, news of a crushing defeat suffered by the Republic at the battle of Agnadello arrived. The battle of Agnadello was the first battle in the War of the League of Crambrai (1508-1516). This war came about as the Papal States under Pope Julius II wanted to curb Venetian influence in northern Italy. The excuse came when the Republic provoked Pope Julius by appointing its own candidate to the vacant Bishopric of Vicenza. In response the Pope called for all Christian to join him in an expedition to subdue Venice. [216] On 10 December 1508, representatives of the Papacy, France, the Holy Roman Empire of Austria, and Spain, joined the League of Cambrai against the Republic.[217] The agreement provided for the complete dismemberment of Venice's territory on the mainland and for its partition among the signatories. Maximilian Holy Roman Empire and Archduke of Austria, in addition to regaining

---

[214] Sanuto, Nei Diarii, Vols VII, VIII, X, 1507, 1508, 1509
[215] ibid
[216] Norwich, J: A History of Venice, Paperback, 18 June 1989 pp. 394–395
[217] Mallet, M and Shaw, C: The Italian Wars, 1494 – 1559, Pearson, 2012, p.87

Gorizia, Trieste, Merania, and eastern Istria, would receive Verona, Vicenza, Padua, and Friuli. Louis XII of France would annex Brescia, Crema, Bergamo, and Cremona to its Milanese possessions. Ferdinand of Spain would seize Otranto. The remainder, including Rimini and Ravenna, would be added to the Papal States.[218] The War of the League of Cambrai commenced on 15 April 1509, with the battle of Agnadello, when the French army under the command of Louis XII left Milan and invaded Venetian territory.[219] To oppose its advance, Venice had amassed a mercenary army near Bergamo. The French surrounded the Venetian troops on three sides and proceeded to destroy the forces over the next three hours. The Venetian cavalry charged the centre of the French Army to relieve the pressure on the infantry. Despite being initially successful, the Venetian cavalry was soon outnumbered, surrounded, and the formation collapsed, with surviving knights fleeing from the battlefield. More than four thousand were killed, including commanders of the Venetian forces, and 30 pieces of artillery were captured.[220] Louis XII proceeded to occupy Venetian territory as far east as Brescia without encountering any significant resistance, with the Venetians losing all the territory that they had accumulated in northern Italy during the previous century.[221] The major cities that had not been occupied by the French, Padua, Verona, and Vicenza were left undefended, and quickly surrendered to Maximilian Holy Roman Empire and Archduke of Austria.[222] Shortly afterwards, Vicenza, Este, Feltre, Belluno and Padua were

---

[218] Shaw, C: Julius II: The Warrior Pope, Blackwell Publishers, Oxford, 1993, pp.228-234

[219] Mallet, M and Shaw, C:The Italian Wars, 1494 – 1559, Pearson, 2012, p.89

[220] ibid

[221] Mallet (n219), p. 400

[222] ibid

restored to Venetian control in a counter attack.[223]

For a moment it seemed Andrea Foscolo would forge an Ottoman-Venetian alliance to join the conflict. However, nothing came of it. The Sultan began to procrastinate, citing political complications with the Wallachians, then an earthquake in the same capital, and finally in 1510 a fire in the royal palace. Famines, revolts, fratricidal fights for the now imminent succession to the throne between the four sons of the Sultan ensued, leading to political paralysis. Andrea finally obtained repatriation in 1512, having become a rich man.[224]

At the time of Andrea Foscolo's return, the Senate was fully engaged on matters closer to home. Pope Julius had become increasingly concerned by the growing French presence on the mainland and had switched sides, allying himself with Venice against Louis XII. The Venetian and Papal alliance eventually expanded into a broader alliance known as the Holy League, which drove the French from Italy in 1512. However, disagreements about the division of the spoils, led Venice to abandon the alliance in favour of one with France in 1513, under the leadership of Francis I, who had succeeded Louis XII to the throne of France.[225] In the same year, Andrea offered money to the homeland for the defence of Padua and Treviso, and a grateful Senate honoured him with election among the wise to the

---

[223] Mallet, M and Shaw, C:The Italian Wars, 1494 – 1559, Pearson, 2012, pp. 405, 406

[224] Gullino, G: Andrea Foscolo, Dizionario Biografico degli Italiani, Vol 49, 1997

[225] Rowland, I: A summer outing in 1510: religion and economics in the papal war with Ferrara, Viator 18, 1987 pp 347–359.

esteemed citizen.[226] The French and Venetians, through victory at the Battle of Marignano in 1515, regained the territory they had lost. The treaties of Noyon and Brussels in 1516, ended the War of Cambrai, which confirmed Venetian claims in all Lombardy except for Cremona, returning to the status quo of 1508.[227] In 1524, Andrea in recognition of his contributions to the Republic, was elected to the very prestigious post of Magistracy of the Supervisors.[228]

In 1517 Andrea Foscolo married Caterina, daughter of Giovanni Frangipane, Count of Veglia and Segna. Venice had annexed the island of Quarnaro in 1480, forcing the Count to reside in Venice and to marry his daughter with a Patrician Francesco Dandolo. When he died of the plague in 1510, Andrea had seen fit to marry his widow, and make Dandalo's dowry his own. The marriage remained sterile and Caterina pre-mourned Andrea, condemning his branch of the family to extinction when he died in 1528.[229]

The brother of the afore mentioned Andrea, **Pietro Foscolo (1448-1523)**, son of Girolamo, entered the Great Council in 1475. A few years later, in 1479, he was elected Governor of Pago (*Conte Pago*). By 1484 Pietro had become a powerful voice in the Senate and was elected one of the Chiefs of the Council of Forty, judging criminal appeals.[230] Later in the same year he became Supervisor of the Merchants (*Sopra consoli dei Mercanti*) judging bankruptcy petitions. In 1485 he was again elected to the

---

[226] Gullino, G: Andrea Foscolo, Dizionario Biografico degli Italiani, Vol 49, 1997
[227] Rowland, I: A summer outing in 1510: religion and economics in the papal war with Ferrara, Viator 18, 1987 pp 347–359.
[228] Gullino (n226)
[229] ibid
[230] Sanuto, Nei Diarii, vol XXXIII, 1522

Council of Forty where he was an elector of Doge Marco Barbarigo. In 1490 he was elected to the post of Governor of Zante, Ionian Islands (*Provveditore di Zante*). He was elected to the same post again several years later in 1501, at the time of the Ottoman War of 1499 to 1503.[231] It was during this term that Pietro conveyed important intelligence to the Senate regarding Ottoman sentiments following their loss of Santa Maura (Modern day Lefkada, Greece).[232] In 1505 Pietro was elected Governor of Kefalonia, Ionian Islands (*Provveditore di Kefalonia*).[233] At the time of his appointment arable lands were being underutilised, and the situation had begun to seriously impact the islands economy. Among other useful proclamations, Pietro declared that those who did not work their lands would be deprived of it. This was applauded by the Senate as an effective measure, which shook even the most indifferent landowners to action. Eventually this hard-line approach helped remedy the Islands economic woes.[234] He returned to the senate in 1513 and was again elected Governor of Kefalonia in 1516.[235] In 1520 Pietro was elected Governor of Canea (*Pòdesta Canea*), modern day Chania, Crete, but his term there did not go beyond the limits of routine. He died heirless in 1523.

The historical record is more muted about the life of **Andrea Foscolo (1425-1475)** son of Paolo, and the first cousin of the afore mentioned brothers Andrea and Petro Foscolo. It is known that in 1447 he served in the internal magistracy, and many years

---

[231] Hope,C: Chroniques Greco-Romanes, Avec Notes et Tables Genealogiques, Berlin, 1873, p.406
[232] Sanuto, Nei Diarii, vol IV, pp. 1501, 1502
[233] Hope, (n231), p.406
[234] Rossi, Geovanni, Reggiment e mss, tomo XVIII
[235] Hope (231), p.406

later in 1465 he was elected a Counsellor in Corfu.[236] In 1470 he was elected Governor of Rovereto[237] and died heirless shortly after.

The Republic once again went to war in 1521, as part of the Fourth Italian War (1521 to 1526). At this time the Foscolo family lineage had progressed to two brothers, Andrea and Zaccaria Foscolo, sons of Marco.

Andrea Foscolo (1470-1528), son of Marco, took his place in the Great Council as soon as he came of age. In 1494 he married Elisabetta Foscari, who brought him a dowry of 4,000 ducats. She was the sister of Marco Foscari, who was to become one of the most powerful Patricians of the Republic. Andrea together with his brother-in-law founded a successful mercantile company.[238] In 1501, Andrea was elected Deputy Governor of Corfu.[239] On his return to Venice, he spent several years in the Senate. Then in 1519, Andrea together with Gabriele Moro, were dispatched as Ambassadors to Ferrara. They were accompanying Madonna Lucrezia Borgia, daughter of Pope Alexander, who had been betrothed to Alfonso, son of The Duke of Ecole. [240] Later that year, Andrea was elected Governor of Crema in Lombardy (*Pòdesta Crema*).[241] Although the City of Crema was considered an outpost, at the time it took on great strategic importance. It was from Crema where Francis I, King of France and Duke of Milan, was preparing to launch his defence against Charles V, The

---

236 Segretario Voci Register 6, folio 78r , 1565
237 Segretario Voci Register 6, folio 61v , 1570
238 Gullino, G: Andrea Foscolo, Dizionario Biografico degli Italiani, Vol 49, 1997
239 Bembo, Storia I, p.283, Sanuto, Nei Diarii, vol iv
240 Sanuto, Nei Diarii, vol iv
241 Sanuto, Nei Diarii, vol xxxiii, 1522

Holy Roman Emperor and Archduke of Austria. Charles V was attempting to gain Milan, Parma, and Piacenza from the Venetian-Franco forces. [242] As war was imminent, Andrea immediately set to work strengthening the city's defences. He collected reliable intelligence on conflict between the Spanish and the French, and received intelligence from Don Giovanni de Medici, also known as Della Bande Nere, the famous military mercenary. This intelligence was reflected in letters he sent to Venice, and to the Administrator of the Venetian Army, Andrea Gritti. War approached in the spring of 1522, and Andrea wrote to the Senate that Giovanni Della Bande Nere, who was allied with Charles V, had told him he was confident of victory against the Venetian-Franco forces.[243] This came to pass, and Andrea described the defeat suffered by the Franco-Venetian troops in two letters to his son Nicolò. The City of Crema however did not fall, and Andrea received praise in the Senate for how he had successfully defended the city under difficult circumstances. [244] After the defeat, Venice used diplomacy to remove itself from the conflict without loss of territory.

In 1523, Andrea was elected to the Council of Forty, and became one of the Fifteen Wise Men responsible for reforming municipal taxes (*Savi di Estimo*).[245] Later that year, Andrea was elected one of the Chiefs of the Council of Forty and was among the electors of Doge Andrea Gritti. A few weeks after this election, Andrea became Governor of Friuli (*Luogotenente della Patria del Friuli*).[246] He took office in October 1523 and kept it for nineteen

---

[242] Gullino, G: Andrea Foscolo, Dizionario Biografico degli Italiani, Vol 49, 1997
[243] Sanuto, Nei Diarii, vol xxxiii, 1522
[244] Gullino, (n242)
[245] Sanuto (n243)
[246] Mss, Sivos, Elezioni di Dogi, e Mss, Reggimenti

months. It was a demanding post, given negotiations on borders between the Republic and Friuli were in progress. Andrea showed skill and diplomacy both in the collection of taxes, and in the delicate negotiations on border matters. On his return to Venice Andrea was elected to the Council of Ten but was unable to take up the position due to ill health.[247] He died in 1528 and was succeeded by his sons, who after a conflict with authorities over their father's medical fitness to serve, moved away from Venice and did not seek election to administrative or military posts.

In the late 16th Century under Doge Andrea Gritti, the erosion of the Republics trade monopoly began. The emergence of European competitors in trade, as well as new trade routes with the East and Americas, was pushing the government towards bankruptcy.[248] Around this critical time, the brother of the afore mentioned Andrea Foscolo, **Zaccaria Foscolo (1468-1540)**, son of Marco, became one of the Five Wise Men of Trade (*Savi Mercanzia*) in 1524, and together with Girolamo Basadonna and Antonio Bembo, was responsible for important reforms to trade, sea routes, and the manning of the Venetian fleet.[249,250]

A few years later in 1536, the Ottoman Sultan Süleyman without notice laid siege to the Venetian Island of Corfu, breaking the peace treaty signed with Venice in 1502 and beginning the Third Ottoman-Venetian War of 1536 to 1540. The Ottomans faced heavy resistance from the Venetians. The siege lasted less than

---

[247] Gullino, G: Andrea Foscolo, Dizionario Biografico degli Italiani, Vol 49, 1997
[248] Fitzsimons, A. K: The political, Economic and Military Decline of Venice leading up to 1797, Thesis, University of North Texas, 2013
[249] Sanuto, Nei Diarii, vol XXXIV, 1524
[250] Cicogna, E: Nelle Nozze Dell Nobile Daulo Augusto Di Foscolo Colla Baronessa Margh Degli Orefic, 1842, p. 14

two weeks. Sultan Süleyman worried by plague among his troops, decided to return home to Constantinople with his fleet. However, in 1538, the Ottomans turned their attention to Venetian possessions in the Aegean, capturing the islands of Skiros, Palmos, Aegina, Ios, Paros, and Astipalia, as well as taking the last two Venetian settlements on the Peloponnese, Malvasia and Naflion.[251] The Ottomans next turned their focus to the Adriatic. Through the combined use of their navy, and their army in Albania, they made significant advances in the Dalmatian hinterland. The Ottomans did not occupy any Venetian cities, but it took the Kingdom of Hungary's Dalmatian possessions, eliminating the buffer zone between the Ottoman and Venetian territory. A humiliated Republic signed a treaty with the Ottoman Empire to end the war on 2 October 1540.[252]

The war with the Ottomans was particularly painful for the Republic. Although the state by this time had regained some financial stability, the loss trading posts squeezed trade revenues further. Trade began to decline sharply from about 1550. Patricians no longer received the same large returns they saw from trade in earlier centuries. Rather than seek profit through other forms of business, they instead sunk their money into land on the mainland and luxury goods. They continued spending as though money flowed freely and still insisted on living a luxurious lifestyle. This worsened the economic situation, and led to resentment from the citizenry, who saw these excesses as proof of social inequality. To rein in the outlandish customs of luxury and fashion, and to try to maintain some semblance of economic and

---

[251] Garnier, E: L'Alliance Impie Editions du Felin, 2008
[252] Hrabak, B: Turske provale i osvajanja na području današnje severne Dalmacije do sredine XVI. stoleća. Journal – Institute of Croatian History, University of Zagreb, 1986

social stability, the Venetian government passed sumptuary laws.[253] **Marco Foscolo (1510-1570)**, Senator son of Zaccarias, in 1562 was elected superintendent for enforcing compliance and execution of the decrees issued in the matter of repression of pomp and excessive luxuries (*Provedadori sora la Parte de le Pompe*). Marco's decrees placed controversial curbs on excessive luxury of weddings, feasts, robes, ornaments, the excessive use of carriages on the mainland, horses, servant numbers, and immoderate decorations of houses and palaces.[254]

From this Marco Foscolo (1510-1570), start the two aristocratic lines of the Foscolo family that extend to the end of the Republic in 1797. These branches begin from the two sons of Marco, Francisco Foscolo (1545-1605) and his brother Zaccaria Foscolo (1538-1603).[255] For convenience, these two branches of the family will be referred to as the San Vio and San Stefano branch respectively. The two brothers flourished in the Senate at a very critical time. It was the end of the 16th Century, and conflict with the Ottomans was imminent. No members of the Foscolo family directly participated in the Fourth Venetian-Ottoman War of 1570 to 1573. However, the family was not untouched by war, and were engaged in key decisions in the Senate.

The Republic had renewed its peace treaty with the Ottomans in 1567.[256,257] However, an excuse was found by the Ottomans to

---

[253] Fitzsimons, A. K: The political, Economic and Military Decline of Venice leading up to 1797, Thesis, University of North Texas, 2013
[254] Sandi, Tentori, VIII, p. 238
[255] Cicogna, E: Nelle Nozze Dell Nobile Daulo Augusto Di Foscolo Colla Baronessa Margh Degli Orefic,1842 p 15
[256] Setton, K.M: The Papacy and the Levant (1204–1571), Volume III, Philadelphia, The American Philosophical Society, 1984 p. 923
[257] McEvedy, C. & Jones, R: Atlas of World Population History, Penguin, 1978 p. 200

breach the treaty. They pointed to a judicial opinion by the Sheikh ul-Islam. He declared breaching the treaty was justified on the pretext that Cyprus in the 7th century was for a very brief period a possession of the Ottoman Empire, and as such was a former land of Islam that had to be retaken.[258,259] In 1570, **Zaccaria Foscolo (1538-1603),** son of Marco, from the San Stefano branch of the family, was elected one of the Chiefs of the Council of Forty,[260] and by virtue of this, was a member of the Signoria, which consisted of the Doge, Ducal Councillors, and Chiefs of the Council of Forty. It was in this year that the Republics Ambassador to Constantinople, Marco Antonio Barbaro, convinced Zaccaria and other members of the Signoria war was imminent. As a result, preparations were made to reinforce the defences of Candia and Cyprus.[261] Later that year, an Ottoman envoy was sent to Venice bearing an ultimatum demanding the immediate cession of Cyprus.[262] This ultimatum was debated by the Signoria, which included Zaccaria Foscolo. Although some voices advocated the cession of the island in exchange for land in Dalmatia and further trading privileges, the ultimatum was categorically rejected.[263]

In July 1570, an Ottoman invasion force landed unopposed near

---

[258] Finkel, C: Osman's Dream: The Story of the Ottoman Empire 1300–1923, John Murray, London, 2006 pp. 158–159
[259] Abulafia, D: The Great Sea: A Human History of the Mediterranean, Penguin, 2012
[260] Sandi, Tentori, VIII
[261] Turnbull, S: The Ottoman Empire 1326–1699, Essential Histories Series 62, Osprey Publishing, 2003. p.58
[262] Finkel (n258) p. 160
[263] Cook, M. A: Cambridge History of Islam and the New Cambridge Modern History, Cambridge University Press, 1976 p. 108

Larnaca, and marched towards the capital Nicosia.[264,265] The siege at Nicosia lasted 45 days until the Ottomans succeeded in breaching the walls of the fortress.[266] A massacre of the city's 20,000 inhabitants ensued. The surviving women and children were rounded up to be sold as slaves. Following the fall of Nicosia, the fortress of Kyrenia in the north of the island surrendered without resistance. The 100,000 strong Ottoman force then marched on Famagusta and laid siege. The 6000 defenders of Famagusta were led by Marco Antonio Bragadin, Captain-General of Famagusta.[267] He was the brother-in-law of the afore mentioned Zaccaria Foscolo (1538-1603).[268] Against all odds the defenders held out for 11 months. However, in 1571, an intensive bombardment of Famagusta's fortifications began, and within 3 months with ammunition and supplies exhausted, the garrison surrendered the city.[269] The Ottoman commander agreed that in return for the city's surrender, all Christians in the city would be guaranteed safe passage to Candia. The evacuation proceeded smoothly. At the formal surrender ceremony Bragadin, together with his senior military aids, offered the vacated city to Ottoman General Lala Mustafa. However, the ceremony turned ugly. The Ottoman General accused Bragadin of murdering Ottoman prisoners and hiding munitions. Without warning, Mustafa pulled a knife and cut off Bragadin's right ear, then ordered his guards to cut off the other ear and his nose, and his senior military

---

264 Turnbull, S: The Ottoman Empire 1326–1699, Essential Histories Series 62, Osprey Publishing, 2003 p. 57
265 Abulafia, D: The Great Sea: A Human History of the Mediterranean, Penguin, 2012 p. 447
266 Setton, K. M: The Papacy and the Levant (1204–1571), Volume III, Philadelphia, The American Philosophical Society, 1984 p. 995
267 Turnbull (n264) pp. 58-59
268 Ugo Foscolo: Sui Sepolcri Carme, XIII, Lugi Guidotte, 1844, p 60
269 Turnbull (n264) pp. 59–60

aids were beheaded on the spot. A massacre of all Christians remaining in the city followed. After being left in prison for two weeks, his earlier wounds festering, Bragadin was dragged round the walls of the fortress with sacks of earth and stone on his back. He was then tied to a chair and hoisted to the yardarm of the Ottoman flagship, where he was exposed to taunts of the Ottoman sailors.[270] Finally, he was taken to his place of execution in the main square, tied naked to a column, and flayed alive. Bragadin suffered in silence as he was skinned alive. Skin was cut from his back, face, arms and thorax. He finally died 30 minutes into the ordeal once his executioner reached his waist. Bragadin's head was severed, and his quartered body was then distributed as a war trophy among the Ottoman army. His skin was stuffed with straw and sewn. Reinvested with his military insignia, his stuffed remains were then exhibited riding an ox in a mocking procession along the streets of Famagusta.[271]

As the horrendous scenes on Famagusta were unfolding, Pope Pius V had concluded a Christian alliance with the Republic, and the Holly League. A combined Christian fleet of 212 galleys, 100 supply vessels, and a force of 50,000 men were on route to Famagusta. The fleet learned of the fate of Famagusta on arrival in Corfu. They rerouted to Lepanto where the 278 strong Ottoman fleet awaited. It is estimated that between 70 to 90 percent of all galleys in existence in the Mediterranean at the time participated in this action.[272] The two evenly matched fleets engaged in battle at Lepanto, at the entrance of the Gulf of -

---

[270] Alvise Zorzi, La République du Lion, Histoire de Venise. p. 220
[271] Norwich, J: A History of Venice, Paperback – Illustrated, 18 June 1989 p. 479
[272] Guilmartin, J. F: Galleons and Galleys: Gunpowder and the Changing Face of Warfare at Sea, 1300–1650 Cassell, 2003 p. 141

Foscolo Family of Venice: Patricans and Aristocrats (A Genealogy)

Colorised Portrait of the Execution of Marco Antonio Bragadin, Anonymous

Corinth. The Christian fleet inflicted a crushing defeat on the Ottomans, with the Ottoman fleet all but destroyed.[273,274,275] The battle was decisive, the Ottomans never regained their naval supremacy in the region. Despite the victory, diverging interests of the League members began to show, and the alliance began to unravel. The Republic, fearing the loss of her Dalmatian possessions, and a possible Ottoman invasion of Friuli, initiated unilateral negotiations. [276,277,278] In 1573 a peace treaty was signed. Cyprus was ceded and became an Ottoman province, the Republic paid an indemnity of 300,000 ducats, and the borders in Dalmatia were modified to reflect Ottoman gains of small but important parts of the hinterland[279]. So ended the tumultuous 16th Century.

17th – 18th Century

The Republic entered the 17th Century in a weak and vulnerable position. Its economy, which had once prospered because of its control over the eastern spice trade, had continued to suffer because of growth in Atlantic trade routes, and greater competition from newly formed trading companies such as the

---

[273] Abulafia, D: The Great Sea: A Human History of the Mediterranean, Penguin, 2012 pp. 450–451
[274] Finkel, C: Osman's Dream: The Story of the Ottoman Empire 1300–1923, John Murray, London, 2006, pp. 160–161
[275] Guilmartin (n254)pp. 141–149
[276] Setton, K.M: The Papacy and the Levant (1204–1571), Volume III, Philadelphia, The American Philosophical Society, 1984 pp. 1093–1095
[277] Finkel (n274) p. 161
[278] Faroqhi, S: The Ottoman Empire and the World Around It, I.B. Tauris, 2004 p. 4
[279] Finkel (n274) p. 161

Dutch East India Company.²⁸⁰

The loss of Cyprus was also felt by the Republic. Together with Candia, it was one of the major overseas possessions. Aside from its location, which allowed control of Levantine trade, the island provided revenues from its production of cotton and sugar.²⁸¹ The commercial decline was accompanied by all the social repercussions, which inevitably follow periods of economic contraction. In the early part of the 17th Century, the Republic was focused largely on trade and economic policies, and the activities in the Senate and civil administration took centre stage.

At the time the Foscolo family were well represented in the Senate. **Marco Foscolo (1579-1630)**, son of Francisco, and his brother **Nicolò Foscolo (1581-1641)**, from the San Vio branch of the family, were both active in the Senate in the early part of the 17th Century. Marco was noted for his eloquence and reasoning, and even in his youth in 1601, delivered several notable speeches on various political questions. ²⁸² **Luigi Foscolo (1560-1623)**, son of Zaccaria, from the San Stefano branch of the family, was a very powerful voice in the Senate at the time. In 1606, he was one of the Chiefs of the Council of Forty, and an elector of Doge Leonardo Donato.²⁸³

The Foscolo family was also well represented in civil administration in the early part of the 17th Century. **Giambattista Foscolo (1588–1643)**, son of Francesco, from

---

280 Finkel, C: Osman's Dream: The Story of the Ottoman Empire 1300–1923, John Murray, London, 2006,pp. 113, 158

281 Faroqhi, S: The Ottoman Empire and the World Around It, I.B. Tauris, 2004 p. 140

282 Cicogna, E: Nelle Nozze Dell Nobile Daulo Augusto Di Foscolo Colla Baronessa Margh Degli Orefic,1842, p.15

283 ibid

the San Vio branch of the family, was in 1631 elected Governor of Candia (*Doge Candia*).[284] This was a challenging assignment, as it came at the end of a serious outbreak of the plague in Venice between 1629 and 1631. The outbreak had killed more than 45,000 people in Venice and had wiped out more than half the population of Parma and Verona. On his arrival in Candia, Giambattista was occupied with plague prevention measures. Although the plague was largely confined to the mainland, the Republic believed in the contagious nature of the disease, and established regulations and practices including quarantine and entry controls to the island.[285] Implementation and enforcement of these practices was not an easy task, as the island's bureaucracy was well known at the time for its lethargy.[286] The outbreak also caused serious disruptions to the islands trade and economy, which demanded Giambattista's attentions in its immediate aftermath. His initiatives earned him appreciation in the Senate on his return to Venice in 1634.[287] A few years later, in 1639, **Marco Foscolo (1584-1644)**, son of Luigi, from the San Stefano branch of the family, also contributed to civil administration when he was elected Governor of Cerigo, Ionian Islands.[288] However, his time on the island did not go beyond the limits of routine. Normalcy had returned following the plague

---

284 Cicoggna, E: Nelle Nozze Dell Nobile Daulo Augusto Di Foscolo Colla Baronessa Margh Degli Orefic,1842, p.15

285 Konstantinidou, K, Mantadakis E, Falaga M, Sardi, T, and Samonis, G: Venetian Rule and Control of Plague Epidemics on the Ionian Islands during 17th and 18th Centuries, Emerg Infect Dis,15(1), 2009 pp.39–43

286 Mason, N.D: The War of Candia, 1645-1669, LSU Historical Dissertations and Theses 235, 1972.

287 Cicogna (n284), p.15

288 Hope, C: Chroniques Greco-Romanes, Avec Notes et Tables Genealogiques, Berlin, 1873

outbreak, and it was a time of peace in the region.

In the mid 17th century, it was **Leonardo Foscolo (1588-1666)**, son of Senator Luigi, from the San Stefano branch of the family, which made the family's greatest contributions to the Republic in the Senate, public administration, and the military.[289] Leonardo entered the Great Council in 1609 but decided to embrace a military career. He became Patron at Arsenal in 1617. Prior to completing his mandate, in 1618 he assumed the post of Captain of the Guards on the Islands of Kvarnern, Istrian coast. Most of Leonardo's time in this role was dedicated to skirmishes with the Uskoks, guerrilla forces sponsored by the Austrians and Spanish to attack the Ottomans, but who often supplemented their incomes through piracy.[290]

In 1619 Leonardo returned to Venice where he was appointed Governor of Prisons. Later that year, Leonardo returned to active service in command of a squadron of galleys patrolling the Aegean, but military problems were slight. It was during this time he became profoundly concerned at the conditions his crews had to suffer. His report on the matter to the Senate gained no sympathy. Instead, he received loud denunciation, and he became the subject of personal attacks. In a letter dated 1619, he hinted at false slanders hatched against his House, and the devastating consequences these had on him. Despite the gossip, in 1620 Leonardo was promoted to Commander of the Adriatic Fleet (*Capitanîo, Golfo*), a position he held for four years.

---

[289] Cicoggna, E: Nelle Nozze Dell Nobile Daulo Augusto Di Foscolo Colla Baronessa Margh Degli Orefic,1842, p.15
[290] Targhetta, R: Leonardo Foscolo, Dizionario Biografico degli Italiani, Volume 49, 1997

Portrait of Leonardo Foscolo, 1653, Anonymous

However, his command did not go beyond the limits of routine.[291]

In 1624, Leonardo Foscolo moved into civil administration, when he was elected Governor of Candia (*Provveditore Candia*). He arrived on the island at the beginning of 1626.[292] It was a difficult assignment, the islands treasuries were drained of funds, officials and military officers received exorbitant salaries, corrupt judges commonly accepted bribes, and even the higher clergy of the island did little to bring credit and honour to Venetian rule. In fact, rule on the island at the time of Leonardo's arrival had become so ineffective, public acts of disorder and violence were commonplace.[293] To try to bring some semblance of good governance and fairhanded objectivity, Leonardo decided to cover the role of both administrator and Judge. His time in the position was spent instructing trials, dealing with the many issues relating to shipwrecks, mediating disputes with the Orthodox clergy, and dealing with bitter conflicts between feudal lords on the island.[294]

Leonardo returned to Venice in 1628 and continued his career in the Senate and public administration. He assumed positions of ever-increasing prestige. In 1628, Leonardo was given responsibility for construction of galleons, and in the same year was elevated to become Administrator of the Venetian Navy. In 1629, Leonardo was elected Administrator of the Courts. Later that year, he was elected in the Senate to the Council of Ten. He resigned from that position in 1630, to take up a two-year

---

291 Targhetta, R: Leonardo Foscolo, Dizionario Biografico degli Italiani, Volume 49, 1997
292 Cornaro, Creta Sacra II, p. 443
293 Mason, N.D: The War of Candia, 1645-1669, LSU Historical Dissertations and Theses 235 ,1972.
294 Cornaro (n292), p. 443

appointment as Governor of the Bank of Venice. He was elected for a second time Administrator of the Venetian Navy in 1632. This was followed in 1633 by his appointment as Governor of the Bank of Piazza. Leonardo was appointed in 1634 as Administrator of Gold and Coins, and later that year became Administrator of Revenues. In 1635 he was elected for a third time Administrator of the Venetian Navy. In the following year the Senate elected Leonardo a member of the Council of Ten. In 1637, Leonardo was elected to the very prestigious post of Magistracy of the Supervisors. The following year in 1638, the Senate elected Leonardo to the Council of Ten for the third time, but he renounced the position to enter the even more powerful Ducal Council. He was then appointed administrator of the Mint in 1640, and later that year Governor of the Revenues for a second time. Leonardo was elected Administrator of Revenues a third time in 1641, and later that year Administrator of the Mint for a second time. In 1643 Leonardo became Administrator of the Arsenal.[295] Shortly after this, in 1644, the Republic found itself in an extremely difficult diplomatic situation.

The Republic, with its now weak military and dependence on uninterrupted trade, was anxious not to provoke the Ottomans, and fastidiously observed the terms of its 1573 peace treaty.[296] However, the pretext for war came in 1644. The Knights of Malta attacked an Ottoman convoy on its way from Constantinople to Alexandria. The convoy was carrying several pilgrims bound for Mecca. Amongst them was the exiled Kızlar Ağa, Chief Black Eunuch, Sünbül Ağa, the Kadi of Cairo, and the nurse of the

---

[295] Targhetta, R: Leonardo Foscolo, Dizionario Biografico degli Italiani, Volume 49, 1997

[296] Finkel, C: Osman's Dream: The Story of the Ottoman Empire 1300–1923, John Murray, London, 2006 p. 222

future Sultan Mehmed IV. During the fight, Sünbül Ağa and most of the important pilgrims were killed. The remaining passengers, 350 men and 30 women, were taken captive to be sold as slaves.[297] The Knights docked at a small harbour on the southern coast of Candia for a few days, where they disembarked several sailors and slaves. The Ottomans became enraged by the incident and accused the Venetians of deliberately colluding with the Knights.[298]

At the time of this diplomatic incident, Leonardo Foscolo was serving on the Council of Ten. He renounced that position and was immediately appointed to the Ducal Council. By virtue of this appointment, he became a member of the Signoria, which consisted of the Doge, Ducal Councillors, and the three chiefs of the Council of Forty. It was the Ducal Council and Signoria that debated and agreed on all decisions concerning the crisis. The Republic strongly denied their involvement in the incident and entered negotiations to avoid a war they could scarcely afford. However, the Ottomans saw the incident as a perfect opportunity for a war against a very much weakened adversary.[299] Despite a long period of negotiations, and several attempts to appease the Ottomans, no diplomatic solution could be found, and so commence the Candia Wars of 1645 to 1669.

The first action of the war came in July 1645. Over 416 vessels and 50,000 troops under the command of Silahdar Yusuf Pasha, the Ottoman Sultan's son-in-law, were dispatched to Candia making

---

[297] Setton, K.M: Venice, Austria and the Turks in the 17th Century, American Philosophical Society ,1991 p. 111
[298] Finkel, C: Osman's Dream: The Story of the Ottoman Empire 1300–1923, John Murray, London, 2006 p. 225
[299] Finlay, G: The History of Greece under Othoman and Venetian Domination, William Blackwood and Sons, London, 1856 p. 128

landfall near Canea. The Ottomans first attacked the small island fortress of San Teodoro. The fortress commander, Biagio Guiliana, realized there was no chance of escape or defence for his garrison of several dozen men. Rather than surrendering to the Ottomans, he ordered the fortress mined. The subsequent explosion destroyed the fortress itself, nearly all the Venetian garrison including Biagio Guiliana, and approximately 150 of the enemy were killed. The Ottomans then marched on Canea and laid siege. It held for 56 days before falling.[300]

The Republic was aware it could not defend itself against the Ottoman onslaught and sought support from other parts of Christendom. Fortunately for the weakened Republic, it was able to obtain military commitments from the Papal States, Tuscany, Malta, and Naples. A Christian fleet was assembled and set sail for Canea. On their arrival they found the Ottoman fleet in total disarray. However, the Christian fleet under the overly cautious command of Niccolò Ludovisi, the Pope's nephew, failed to exploit the opportunity. When he finally moved to retake Canea in October 1645, with a fleet of about 90 ships, the attack failed.[301]

A few months earlier, in July 1645, the Senate anticipating an Ottoman invasion of Dalmatia, had elected Leonardo Foscolo Governor of Dalmatia (*Provveditore Dalmatia*). Military command of the territory went to Andrea Vendramin. Dalmatia was of great strategic importance to the Republic. The territory shared a common land border with the Ottoman Empire, and it was near the Venetian mainland. However, a mountainous barrier between the Venetian held coastal areas and Ottoman

---

[300] Setton, K.M: Venice, Austria and the Turks in the 17th Century, American Philosophical Society, 1991 p. 127
[301] ibid, p.128-129

held interior, as well as its waterways and channels, made Dalmatia one of the Republics most easily defended overseas territories. [302]

The Ottoman invasion of Dalmatia came in December 1645.[303] Despite the natural defences of the territory, on this occasion the Republics defence went very poorly. The fortresses at Novegradi and Scardonia fell to a sizable Ottoman Army. Hapless attempts by Andrea Vendramin and his forces to recapture both forts failed and merely emboldened Ottoman resolve. In as little as four months, by the end of April 1646, Ottoman forces controlled an area comprising several thousand square miles between Novegradi and Sebenico.[304,305]

In 1646, a very much demoralized Republic, appointed Leonardo Foscolo both General and Governor of Dalmatia, replacing the weak and irresolute Andrea Vendramin.[306] In Leonardo Foscolo, the Venetian forces were unified under a determined and astute commander. Further unity was accomplished when Leonardo placed the naval forces under his direct command.[307]

Throughout 1646, Leonardo Foscolo made meticulous military preparations. There were the typical shortages of money and supplies to overcome, but by September of 1646, Foscolo had ensured all Venetian fortresses in Dalmatia had been readied for

---

302 Mason, N.D: The War of Candia, 1645-1669, LSU Historical Dissertations and Theses 235 ,1972.
303 Targhetta, R: Leonardo Foscolo, Dizionario Biografico degli Italiani, Volume 49, 1997
304 Anticanto, S: Frammenti Istorici Della Guerra in Dalmazia, Venezia, 1649
305 Sassi, F: Le Campagne di Dalmazia durante la Guerra di Candia (1645-1648), Archivio Veneto, 20,1937
306 Praga, G: Storia di Dalmazia, Pisa, Giardini,1993
307 Mason (note 302)

war. It was now Leonardo Foscolo, assisted by French mercenary, Gil D'As, and the Vicenza based mercenary Enrico Capra, with an army of just 5000 men, that faced a 20,000 strong Ottoman Army. [308] What followed was a series of highly successful defensive and offensive campaigns under Foscolo's brilliant leadership.

In early 1647, favoured by a relatively harsh winter in Dalmatia, which hindered the movement of Ottoman supplies, General Foscolo took the initiative to make his move. Outnumbered on the ground four to one, Leonardo utilized Venetian naval superiority with expertise. He had an army of three thousand infantry and a hundred cavalry transported by sea to the walls of Novegradi, with relative ease and speed. Simultaneously another Venetian force left the Dalmatian capital, Zara, and travelled by land to the ancient Ottoman fortress of Zemonico. This skilfully executed pincer movement by Foscolo neutralize the enemy. In March 1647, Zemonico was gained by the Venetians, and Novegradi retaken. The losses stalled Ottoman momentum, and by the end of 1647 both Vrane and Nadin were retaken by Foscolo's victorious armies, making complete the Republic's victory in the north.[309,310]

General Foscolo then directed his attention to the south and the Ottoman held fortresses of Scardona and Dernis along the Canal of Sebenico. The attack on Scardona brought Foscolo triumph within a few days. However, the Ottoman forces now concentrated in the south, were amassing troops for a serious -

---

[308] Praga, G: Storia di Dalmazia, Pisa, Giardini,1993
[309] Mason, N.D: The War of Candia, 1645-1669, LSU Historical Dissertations and Theses 235 ,1972
[310] Verdi il Libretto sottoindicato: Presa di Clissa, 1648

Foscolo Family of Venice: Patricans and Aristocrats (A Genealogy)

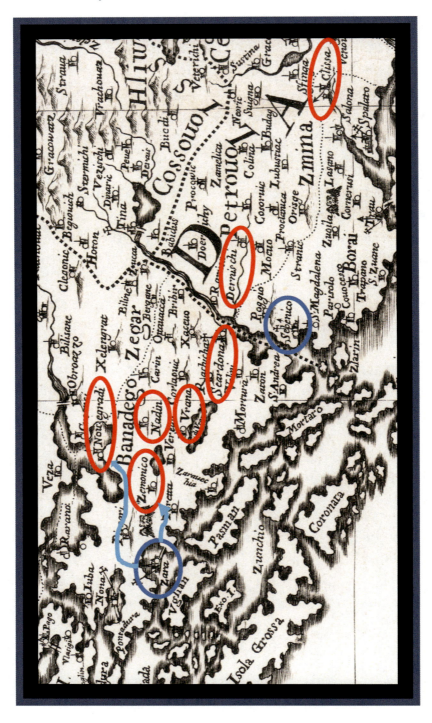

counterattack at the Venetian fort of Sebenico. General Foscolo realised if the attack on Sebenico succeeded, Venetian communications from the coast all the way to Scardona would have been ruptured. Furthermore, the loss of Sebenico would have also meant the loss of control of the Canal of Sebenico and would have denied Venetian forces access to the interior. Foscolo had nearly 3500 infantry and cavalry troops transported to Sebenico in preparation for an Ottoman attack. Tensions mounted as money ran short and the fear of an imminent attack increased amongst the troops causing some French units to rebel. When the attack finally came in August 1647, it proved difficult to repel. Ottoman trenches approached the walls of the fort, and batteries pounded its walls. As sections of the outer defensive perimeter started to crumble, additional Ottoman reinforcements arrived from the East. The situation seemed grim. However ,Foscolo remained calm and swiftly assembled reinforcements, and again used the Navy to transport them along the coast of the Adriatic to Sebenico. This ability to shift forces from one point to another without delay, once again brought victory, and in this case, saved Sebenico. The arrival of additional Venetian units forced the enemy to lift the siege of Sebenico and flee eastward in the direction of Dernis and Chi. Although nearly 6,000 Ottoman troops were hastily assembled at Dernis and Chi, victory went to Foscolo, and the forts were regained by the Venetians in February 1648. [311,312,313]

In spring of 1648 only one fortress of any major importance in

---

[311] Mason, N.D: The War of Candia, 1645-1669, LSU Historical Dissertations and Theses 235 ,1972.
[312] Verdi il Libretto sottoindicato: Presa di Clissa, 1648
[313] Cicogna, E: Nelle Nozze Dell Nobile Daulo Augusto Di Foscolo Colla Baronessa Margh Degli Orefic,1842, p.16

Portrait of General Foscolo with Sebenico in the background, Jacopo Pinccini

Dalmatia remained in control of the Ottoman armies, Clissa. The fortress was located on top of a steep mountain and was impregnable. However, following a two-week siege by Leonardo's troops it too fell in March 1648. One bloody tragedy marred this last great Venetian victory in Dalmatia. The trouble came in Clissa, when the Morlacchi and Polissani tribesmen who had taken part in the siege broke out into a hysterical display of brutality and cruelty against the survivors of the Ottoman garrison. The bitterness generated by three years of warfare with the Ottomans erupted into an uncontrollable massacre. Regardless of attempts to enforce order, even by General Foscolo himself, they continued to ravish and murder with concern neither "for sex nor age".[314] Some to escape the fury threw themselves from windows of the fort to their death. Nonetheless, nothing could detract from the fact that in a relatively short period of time Leonardo Foscolo and his army managed to expel the Ottomans from Novegradi, Zemonico, Clissa, Scardona, Vrana, and Dernis and Chi. In less than two years not a single fortress within sixty-five kilometres of the coast remained in the hands of the Ottomans. With its newly organized army, and the decisive and unquestioned leadership provided by Leonardo Foscolo, the Venetian Republic had swept the enemy from the field and had scored a triumph that would remain unequalled throughout the entire Candian war.[315]

The Senate in 1648 conferred on Leonardo Foscolo the title of "benefactor of the fatherland", passing over voices that accused -

---

[314] Mason, N.D: The War of Candia, 1645-1669, LSU Historical Dissertations and Theses 235 ,1972
[315] ibid

Portrait of General Foscolo with the fort of Clissa in the background, Anonymous

him of extreme rigor and harshness not only towards the enemy, but also against his own men. In war however, results count, and these were positive for Leonardo, thanks to the genuine respect he enjoyed amongst his troops, the intelligent use of the fleet in support of land operations, and his preparedness to use drastic actions against his enemies, including poisoning their wells.[316] In that year Leonardo was elected for a life term to the very prestigious office of the Procurator of San Marco. The office was second only to the Doge in terms of prestige.[317,318]

Meanwhile the war with the Ottomans in the Candian theatre was not progressing well. The Senate had initially appointed the 80-year-old Doge Francesco Erizzo as Captain General of the Sea (*Capitanîo Generale da Mar*), the war time Commander-in-Chief of the Venetian Navy. However, following his death in early 1646, he was replaced by the 73-year-old Giovanni Cappello.[319] Cappello's performance in 1646 had been very poor. He failed to prevent the arrival of Ottoman reinforcements,[320] and his attack on the Ottoman fleet at Canea Bay had failed, as did his attempt to break the Ottoman blockade of Rethymno. As a result, the city fell.[321] In 1647 Ottoman success paved the way for Gazi Hüseyin Pasha, the local commander, to conquer the eastern half of the island, except for the fortress of Siteia.[322] By the beginning of

---

[316] Targhetta, R: Leonardo Foscolo, Dizionario Biografico degli Italiani, Volume 49, 1997
[317] Mason, N.D: The War of Candia, 1645-1669, LSU Historical Dissertations and Theses 235 ,1972
[318] Targhetta (n316)
[319] Setton, K.M: Venice, Austria and the Turks in the 17th Century, American Philosophical Society ,1991 p. 129
[320] Setton, K.M: Venice, Austria and the Turks in the 17th Century, American Philosophical Society ,1991 p.140
[321] ibid, p.141
[322] Ibid p.147

1648, the entire island, except the main fort of Candia and a few strongholds like the island of Gramvousa, was in Ottoman hands.[323] An Ottoman siege began in May 1648, to gain the remaining cities. Giovanni Cappello had been replaced as Captain General of the Sea by Alvise Mocenigo, and the situation improved somewhat. Although he could not directly confront the large Ottoman expeditionary force on Candia, his strategy was to disrupt Ottoman supplies to the island. This succeeded and prevented the Ottomans from making any further gains.[324]

It was at this low point in the War that Leonardo Foscolo wrote to the Council of Ten to propose a plan to end the siege of Candia. This involved infecting Ottoman forces with a poisonous liquid that he described as the quintessence of the plague. The poisonous liquid was produced by a physician known to Foscolo, Michiel Angelo Salamon. It was obtained from a distillate of the spleen, the buboes, and carbuncles of plague victims. Foscolo suggested lacing cloth goods with the poison, and conveying these to Candia where the vessels would be abandoned so the cloth would be hawked to the Ottomans. This would ensure the poisoned cloth passed through as many hands as possible giving the impression of a widespread outbreak of the plague. The Inquisitor of the Council of Ten wrote back to Foscolo thanking him for his plan and agreeing that Salamon should be appointed to produce the poison. The plan was never carried out but shows the determination of Foscolo to do whatever was necessary to prevail, even though his letter displays a great deal of moral

---

[323] Finkel, C: Osman's Dream: The Story of the Ottoman Empire 1300–1923, John Murray, London, 2006 p. 227

[324] Setton, K.M: Venice, Austria and the Turks in the 17th Century, American Philosophical Society, 1991 p. 158-159

anguish to the plan.³²⁵

In 1650, Leonardo Foscolo was elected Captain General of the Sea (*Capitanîo Generale da Mar*), replacing Alvise Mocenigo.³²⁶ He sailed to Candia where he took up his command in August 1651. The Venetian strategy did not foresee decisive operations for that year. Leonardo decided to take the whole fleet to sea in search of the enemy, reaching Chios five days later. However, the Ottoman galleys which were stationed in Chios had already departed for Rhodes. He then sailed to the Ottoman Island of Samos to collect tribute, and when it was refused, landed troops, and ravaged the city. Foscolo then set sail for the Ottoman held islands of Kos and Leros, failing to take the town of Stanchio in the former island, but meeting no great resistance in the latter. Then, feeling that it was too late in the year to do anything against the Ottoman vessels at Rhodes, he went back to Candia for the winter. Shortly after Foscolo had left the area, Ali Pasha returned to Constantinople with 22 galleys, leaving the rest of his fleet in Rhodes.³²⁷

The next two years were comparatively uneventful. Early in 1652 Foscolo's fleet set sail for the Dardanelles, levying tribute in Skyro on the way. Just as he reached the Island of Imbros a gale came on. Although only one galley was lost, enough damage was done to make it necessary to return to Candia. At the beginning of June 1652, Foscolo sailed again for the Dardanelles. He rendezvoused at the Venetian Island of Cerigo with seven Maltese galleys. While

---

325 State archives of Venice. Inquisitors of the State, b. 274, 5 Feb, 18 Mar, 10, 29 Apr, 14, 18 Oct, 1 Dec 1650, 3 Aug 1651.
326 Setton, K.M: Venice, Austria and the Turks in the 17th Century, American Philosophical Society ,1991 pp. 158-159
327 Anderson, R.C: Naval Wars in the Levant 1559-1853, Princeton 1952, 5p.144,145

he was on the way, the Ottomans began to move. An English ship in Venetian service, the Relief of London, on her way to join Foscolo's fleet at the Dardanelles had the misfortune to run into the twenty-six Ottoman galleys between Tenedos and Mitylene. Lack of wind made escape impossible and after a long action her crew set her ablaze to prevent capture. Following this success Karadan Pasha went on southwards and attacked the Venetian Island of Tine (Tinos). Foscolo leaving part of the fleet with his second in command, Barbaro, in the Dardanelles, began to pursue the Ottomans. At the Island of Tine he capture the galley of the Bey of Malvasia, but the rest of the Ottoman fleet were able to escape to Rhodes. Foscolo's fleet then cruised in the Aegean in detachments, capturing an Ottoman galley off Chios and levying tribute in Skiathos on the opposite side of the Aegean.[328] Foscolo then made his way to Suda, Candia, where he captured Armirò, a new fort built by the Ottomans to improve communication between their garrisons at Canea and Rethymno.[329] So ended a relatively successful year for Foscolo. As winter approached, Barbaro had to withdraw from the Dardanelles. Once he had left, the Kapudan Pasha returned to Constantinople without opposition, though he left the bulk of his galleys in Chios.[330]

In spring 1653 Foscolo had to wait for reinforcements from Venice, and when the fleet set sail, it was too late. The Kapudan Pasha was already at Chios, and by the time the Venetians arrived the Ottoman fleet had left for Rhodes. Foscolo headed for Rhodes, but the Pasha declined to engage despite having a superior

---

[328] Setton, K.M: Venice, Austria and the Turks in the 17th Century, American Philosophical Society ,ibid, pp.145, 146
[329] Cicogna, E: Nelle Nozze Dell Nobile Daulo Augusto Di Foscolo Colla Baronessa Margh Degli Orefic,1842, p.17
[330] Anderson, R.C: Naval Wars in the Levant 1559-1853, Princton 1952, p.146

number of vessels. Bombardment by Foscolo's division of 13 sailing ships, and even a landing on the island had no effect. All Foscolo could do was to remain on watch, lying for the most part off the neighbouring islands of Piscopia (Tilos) and Nisyros. Another bombardment produced little effect and the fleet returned to Piscopia. The Kapudan Pasha started for Candia, but by some mischance or mismanagement Foscolo knew nothing. Then, to make matters worse, Foscolo worked slowly round the Aegean instead of going direct to Candia. Finally, Foscolo learnt that the enemy had been in Candian waters for the best part of a month. He immediately set sail and on reaching Canea began a blockade, but the Ottomans found the opportunity to flee unhindered to Constantinople, picking up the rest of their fleet from Rhodes on the way.[331] Foscolo then turned his sights to Malvasia in the province of Morea (modern day Peloponnese), a place of great importance to the Ottomans. He decided to launch a surprise attack. The fort at Malvasia was courageously attacked by Foscolo, but the Ottomans detonated their munitions store and killed many of the Venetian militia. Following this incident Foscolo withdrew from the engagement.[332,333] Leonardo troubled by continuous fevers and migraines had to return to Candia.[334] He spent the last year of his command reinforcing the defences of Candia, then went to Cerigo (Modern day Kythira, Greece), where in June 1654 he handed over to his successor Alvise Mocenigo.[335]

Leonardo Foscolo's performance as Captain General of the Sea was adequate, but unremarkable. However, on his return in 1654,

---

[331] Anderson, R.C: Naval Wars in the Levant 1559-1853, Princton 1952, p.147
[332] Nadi Storia Veneta, II, p.316
[333] Cicogna, E: Nelle Nozze Dell Nobile Daulo Augusto Di Foscolo Colla Baronessa Margh Degli Orefic,1842, p.17
[334] Anderson, R.C: Naval Wars in the Levant 1559-1853, Princton 1952, p.147
[335] ibid

Venice needed heroes, and he still represented the liberator of Dalmatia. He sought election as Doge on four occasions, failing on each ballot despite strong support from the public.[336] In fact, public support was so strong, especially amongst the troops he had commanded, that the Council of Ten asked Leonardo to retire for a time for fear of a popular rebellion. Accusations of abuse of public funds entrusted to him, hindered both his political career and candidacies for Doge. These accusations were never followed up, but the suspicions cost Leonardo the post of Doge. He settled for other lower albeit prestigious appointments until his death in 1666.[337]

Leonardo Foscolo was not the only family member to distinguish himself in the Candian War. **Francesco Foscolo (1604-1664)** the brother of Leonardo, also saw active service in the Dalmatian theatre.[338] He participated in the battle at Zemonico against the Ottomans in 1647. Francesco served as a cavalry officer under the command of Marc Antonnio Pisani, supervisor of the cavalry. Francesco, "greedy no less for danger than for glory", had volunteered to accompany Pisani at great risk to himself and fought valiantly. He returned to Venice at the end of the Dalmatian campaign and served in the Senate.[339]

In 1667 Candia finally fell after a siege that lasted 28 months. Over 108,000 Ottomans and 29,088 Christians lost their lives in the final action. These casualties included 280 Venetian Patricians, a figure equivalent to roughly a quarter of the Great

---

[336] Cicogna, E: Nelle Nozze Dell Nobile Daulo Augusto Di Foscolo Colla Baronessa Margh Degli Orefic,1842), p.18

[337] Targhetta, R: Leonardo Foscolo, Dizionario Biografico degli Italiani, Volume 49, 1997

[338] Cicogna (n336), p.18

[339] ibid

Council.[340] Faced with the renewed Ottoman assault and a struggling economy, in 1669 the Signoria ended the war with a peace settlement with the Ottomans.[341] The surrender ended the four and a half centuries of Venetian rule in Candia (modern day Crete). The cost and casualties incurred during this prolonged war started the decline of the Ottoman Empire.[342] However, the Republic also incurred significant damage due to the war. It lost its greatest and most prosperous colony, its trading position in the Mediterranean was seriously undermined,[343] and its treasury was exhausted having spent more than 4,000,000 ducats on the defence of Candia alone.[344]

A few years later, in 1683, a new war broke out between Austria and the Ottomans. A large Ottoman army advanced to Vienna and laid siege. The Ottoman siege was broken in the battle of Vienna by the King of Poland.[345] As a result, an anti-Ottoman Holy League was formed at Linz on 5 March 1684 between Emperor Leopold I of Austria, King Sobieski of Poland, and Marcantonio Giustinian the Doge of Venice.[346] The Austrians and Poles considered Venetian participation in the war useful, as its navy could impede the Ottomans from concentrating their forces

---

[340] Venezia e il Levante (sec XV - sec XVIII), VENIVA consortium, 1996
[341] Setton, K.M: Venice, Austria and the Turks in the 17th Century, American Philosophical Society ,1991 p. 206
[342] Lewis, B: The Central Islamic Lands from Pre-Islamic Times to the First World War, Cambridge University Press, 1978, p. 631
[343] Mason, N.D: The War of Candia, 1645-1669, LSU Historical Dissertations and Theses 235 ,1972.
[344] Miller, W: Essays on the Latin Orient. Cambridge, Cambridge University Press, 1921, p. 196
[345] Chasiotis, I: History of the Greek Nation, Volume XI: Hellenism under Foreign Rule (Period 1669 - 1821), Ekdotiki Athinon, 1975, pp.14-16
[346] Setton, K.M: Venice, Austria and the Turks in the 17th Century, American Philosophical Society ,1991, p.272

by sea.[347] The Republic saw it as an opportunity to reconquer its lost territories in the Aegean and Dalmatia, at a time when the Ottomans were weakened from their recent loss in Austria, and its forces were distracted fighting the Austrians and Poles in Central Europe. On 5 April 1684, the Republic declared war on the Ottomans for the first time in its history, and so began the Sixth Ottoman Venetian War (1684-1698). [348]

At the outbreak of the Six Ottoman Venetian War the military forces of the Republic were meagre. The long Candian War had exhausted Venetian resources, and Venetian power was in decline on the mainland as well as in the Adriatic. Venice received considerable subsidies from Pope Innocent XI, who played a leading role in forming the Holy League. They also raised funds by selling state offices and titles of nobility.[349] Financial and military aid in men and ships was secured from the Knights of Malta, the Duchy of Savoy, the Papal States and the Knights of St. Stephen of Tuscany, and experienced Austrian officers were seconded to the Venetian army. The Republic enrolled large numbers of mercenaries from Italy and the German states, especially Saxony and Brunswick. [350]

The war went very well for the Republic. Commander-in-Chief of the Venetian forces, Francesco Morosini, in 1684 successfully captured the Island of Santa Maura, Ionian islands (modern day Lefkada), and by 1687 had taken complete control of Morea

---

[347] Setton, K.M: Venice, Austria and the Turks in the 17th Century, American Philosophical Society ,1991, p.272

[348] ibid

[349] Topping, P: Venice's Last Imperial Venture", Proceedings of the American Philosophical Society, 120 (3),1976

[350] Chasiotis, I: History of the Greek Nation, Volume XI: Hellenism under Foreign Rule (Period 1669 - 1821), Ekdotiki Athinon, 1975, p.19

(Peloponnese).[351] After the victories in Morea, Morosini decided to campaign in Central Greece, especially against the Ottoman strongholds of Thebes and Negropont (Chalkis). Athens fell to the Venetians briefly in 1688, where the Parthenon was famously destroyed. Used as a munitions store by the Ottomans, the Parthenon was hit by Venetian artillery unleashing a massive explosion. Athens was regained by the Ottomans a few months later.[352] Despite all efforts in Thebes and Negropont Venetian gains on the Greek mainland did not go beyond Morea. However, the Dalmatia campaign went well, and by 1690 the Republic controlled most of Dalmatia.[353] In 1692, a Venetian fleet under Domenico Mocenigo, attacked and laid siege to Candia, while at the same time the Christians of the island revolted against the Ottomans, but this attempt to retake Candia failed.[354]

The Foscolo family did not participate in the early years of the war. However, in the late 1690s, the war shifted to a series of naval campaigns. **Nicolò Foscolo (1670-1703)**, son of Francesco, of the San Vio branch of the family was involved in the naval campaigns in the Aegean at the end of the Sixth Ottoman Venetian War.[355,356] These campaigns sought to frustrate Ottoman fleet movements in the region, and if possible, force a decisive naval engagement to fatally weaken the Ottoman fleet. In

---

[351] Chasiotis, I: History of the Greek Nation, Volume XI: Hellenism under Foreign Rule (Period 1669 - 1821), Ekdotiki Athinon, 1975, p.26
[352] ibid, pp. 27, 28
[353] Nazor, A: Inhabitants of Poljica in the War of Morea (1684–1699), Croatian Institute of History. 21 (21), 2002 pp.52, 53
[354] Topping, P: Venice's Last Imperial Venture", Proceedings of the American Philosophical Society, 120 (3),1976
[355] Cicogna, E: Nelle Nozze Dell Nobile Daulo Augusto Di Foscolo Colla Baronessa Margh Degli Orefic,1842, p.18
[356] Locatelli, Storia della Guerra in Levante, II, p 161

1696, Nicolo Foscolo was in command of a first rate 60-gun man-of-war, Rosa, under Bartolomeo Contarini, who was in command of sailing ships.[357] On 22 August 1696, Nicolo Foscolo's ship Rosa, together with the Venetian fleet of 22 sailing ships and 19 Galleys, engaged the 40 ship Ottoman fleet at the Naval Battle of Andros. The engagement lasted 2 hours. The Ottomans withdrew, and no ships were lost.[358] In the following year 1697, again under the command of Bartolomeo Contarini, Nicolo Foscolo was in command of a first rate 66-gun man-of-war, Tigre, and saw action in the North Aegean.[359] On 6 July 1697, the 26 strong Venetian fleet, including Nicolo Foscolo's Tigre, engaged the 40 ships of the Ottoman fleet at the Naval Battle of Lemnos. The engagement lasted fifteen hours and the Ottomans lost 3 ships, with their flagship badly damaged.[360] On 20 September 1697, the Venetian fleet was in waters between Castel Rosso and Zea (Keos), when they again encountered the Ottomans. The Ottoman fleet was attacked by a line of 16 Venetian ships, including Nicolo Foscolo's Tigre. After about an hour the Ottomans withdrew. On this occasion the Ottomans suffered severe damage to 3 flagships.[361] In the last campaign of the war in 1698, Nicolo Foscolo was assigned command of the first rate 70-Gun Man-of-War, Amazzone, under Daniele Dolfin.[362] On 16 September 1698, Nicolo Foscolo's Amazzone was with the 26 strong Venetian fleet when they encountered the Ottomans at the Island of Imbros. The Venetian fleet pursued the Ottomans back into the Dardanelles,

---

[357] Cicogna, E: Nelle Nozze Dell Nobile Daulo Augusto Di Foscolo Colla Baronessa Margh Degli Orefic,1842, p.18
[358] Anderson, R.C: Naval Wars in the Levant 1559-1853, Princton 1952, pp.223-225
[359] Cicogna (n357), p.19
[360] Anderson, (n358), pp.229-230
[361] ibid
[362] Cicogna (n357), p.19

and during their efforts to escape, one Ottoman ship was de-mast and one Ottoman flagship was wrecked.[363] Two days later, Nicolo Foscolo's Amazzone again engaged the Ottoman Fleet in the Naval Battle of Samothrace. On this occasion the Ottomans managed to manoeuvre into a position behind the Venetian fleet. There was only one thing Dolfin could do, turn his fleet into the Ottomans and attack. The engagement instantly became a melée. Dolfin's flagship, the Rizzo d'Oro, as it turned collided with another ship, the S.Lorenzo Giustinian, and fell off among the enemy. She was heroically relieved by the Aurora, commanded by Duodo, the Aquila Valiera, commanded by Bonvicini, and Nicolo Foscolo's Amazzone. The Amazzone was the leading ship of the line and was damaged, her steering gear disabled. For some time, she was surrounded by the enemy, but showing great skill and seamanship Foscolo managed to escape.[364]

Although the Venetians were victorious in each Naval engagement, none of the naval campaigns towards the end of the war proved decisive or changed the balance of naval power to any significant extent.[365] However, on his return to Venice in 1698, Nicolo Foscolo received applause from the Senate for his service, and was rewarded with election to the post of Governor of Zante, Ionian Islands.[366] Coming as it did at the end of the war, the post did not go beyond the limits of routine.

In January 1699, the Treaty of Karlowitz was signed between the Ottomans and the Holy League, ending the Sixth Ottoman Venetian War. As part of the peace agreement, the Republic

---

363 Anderson, R.C: Naval Wars in the Levant 1559-1853, Princton 1952, p. 235
364 ibid, pp. 235-236
365 ibid p.236
366 Graziani, Historia Veneta, II, Pp 659, 689, 714

regained all of Morea together with the island of Aegina, as well as kept all gains in Dalmatia[367].

18th – 19th Century

At the beginning of the 18th Century, the Republic had been in a state of decline for over 300 years. Sensing the weakness, the Ottomans had been looking for an opportunity to reverse their losses from the Sixth-Ottoman Venetian War, especially the loss of Morea. The pretext for war came with the Republic's seizure of an Ottoman ship, which had been carrying treasure of the former Grand Vizier, Damad Hasan Pasha, and the Republic's grant of sanctuary to Danilo I, the Prince-Bishop of Montenegro, who had launched an unsuccessful revolt against the Ottomans. In December 1714, the Ottomans declared war on the Republic and the Seventh Ottoman-Venetian War began. [368,369]

At the time of the War Venice's major overseas possession was Morea (Peloponnese). The Ottomans quickly took the Venetian islands of Tinos and Aegina and moved to the mainland to take Corinth. Commander of the Venetian fleet, Daniele Dolfin, rather than risk his fleet held back, and by the time of his engagement with the Ottomans, Naflion, Modon, Coron and Malvasia had all fallen. San Maura in the Ionian islands, and the Venetian bases of Spinalonga and Suda on Candia (Crete) were all abandoned. The Ottomans finally landed on Corfu, but the Venetian defences

---

[367] Finlay, G: The History of Greece under Othoman and Venetian Domination, William Blackwood and Sons, London, 1856 p. 234
[368] Lane, F: Venice, a maritime republic, Johns Hopkins U Press, 1973, p. 411
[369] Setton, K.M: Venice, Austria and the Turks in the 17th Century, American Philosophical Society ,1991, pp. 426–42

held.370

In the summer of 1715, the pasha of Bosnia marched against the Venetian possessions in Dalmatia, with an army of 40,000 men, and laid siege to the town of Sinij. This Siege failed, but the Ottoman threat to Dalmatia was of great concern to the Austrians. The Austrian Emperor Charles VI, with financial support from Pope Clement XI, and with France guaranteeing Austrian possessions in Italy, renewed its alliance with the Republic. As a result, the Ottomans declared war on Austria on 13 April 1716. The threat of the Austrians forced the Ottomans to direct their forces away from Venetian possessions, with the Ottomans suffering a grave defeat at the hands of the Austrians at Petrovaradin on 3 August 1716. Even with momentum very much in their favour, Venetian naval efforts in the Aegean and the Dardanelles in 1717 and 1718 met with little success. The Treaty of Passarowitz signed on 21 July 1718, handed Austria a large territorial gain, but Venice lost Morea in exchange for insignificant gains in Albania and Venetian Dalmatia. So ended the last Venetian-Ottoman war.371

No member of the Foscolo family participated in the last Venetian Ottoman War. While well respected, in the 18th Century most family members were confined to the Senate, Councils, and modest posts in the internal magistracies and administrative offices. At this time Venice was in a rapid state of decline. Genoa gained increasing prominence as a trading port. Livorno, a new port on the Tyrrhenian Sea was created by the Grand Duke of

---

370 Finlay, G: The History of Greece under Othoman and Venetian Domination, William Blackwood and Sons, London, 1856 p. 272-274
371 Setton, K.M: Venice, Austria and the Turks in the 17th Century, American Philosophical Society ,1991, pp. 449-450

Tuscany and became the staging-post for all British trade in the Mediterranean. More damaging perhaps was the Papal town of Ancona and the Habsburg town of Trieste. Ancona took most of the Levant and eastern trade away from Venice, while Trieste took the trade from Germany and the West.[372]

It was in this era of decline that **Francesco Foscolo (1666 – 1726),** son of Alvise, from the San Stefano branch of the family, was elected Governor of Bergamo (*Pòdesta Bergamo*) in 1702. A few years later, in 1712, he was elected Governor of Brescia. On his return to Venice, he became a powerful voice in the Senate. He was a man highly regarded for his intelligence and was highly decorated. Some wrongly believe that the nobility of the San Stefano branch of the Foscolo family, from which the great General Leonardo Foscolo hails, ends with this Francisco. However, he was succeeded by his son Leonardo Foscolo.[373]

Leonardo Foscolo (1693-1753)[374], son of Francesco, from the San Stefano branch of the family, entered the Great Council, but did not hold any positions of note. He established a trading business in Paramizia (modern day Paramythia, Greece). There he married Lena Stratti in 1738. She was the daughter of one of the preeminent families of Paramizia. At the time nobility as a birth right was conferred on children of noble parents. However, it was required to show offspring were conceived within a legal marriage, and that the mother was "of honest condition and not of plebeian background". Even if offspring were legitimate, those descended from mothers of a lower social rank (morganatic

---

372 Norwich, J: A History of Venice, Paperback, 18 June 1989, p. 591
373 Cicogna, Emmanuele: Nelle Nozze Dell Nobile Daulo Augusto Di Foscolo Colla Baronessa Margh Degli Orefic,1842, Pp 10, 27
374 ibid

descendants) were excluded from the line of succession. Marriages to women outside Venetian nobility, required proof of wedding contracts, and had to be investigated and checked by a special nobility magistrate within the public prosecutor's office (*Avogadori di Commun*) to ensure the bride met the standards required for registration in the Golden Book. In the case of Leonardo, evidence of the marriage was presented, and within the 5-year period prescribed, the nobility magistrate found it met all requisites required, allowing the children of the marriage to acquire Venetian nobility. As noted by Cicogna, this information was inscribed in the Golden book, but as Leonardo did not involve himself to any great extent in the Great Council, it was not widely known until the early 19th Century, leading to false conclusions that the San Stefano branch of the family lost nobility. This of course was not the case, and Leonardo was succeeded by his son Francesco.[375]

The Republic by the late 18 Century was in a serious state of decline, with trade on the verge of collapse. In December 1779 reforms were proposed in the Great Council by Giorgio Pisani. These aimed to remove a monopoly of power enjoyed by a small number of rich Patricians to the advantage of a very large number of poor ones. The proposal caused much controversy. Doge Paolo Renier openly opposed the proposal, and sensing a possible insurrection, the Council of Ten took preventative steps confining Pisani to the Castle of San Felice in Verona.[376] A few years later in May 1784 Andrea Tron, known as "the Patron" because of his political influence, summed up the dire situation in a speech to

---

[375] Cicogna, Emmanuele: Nelle Nozze Dell Nobile Daulo Augusto Di Foscolo Colla Baronessa Margh Degli Orefic,1842, Pp 10, 27
[376] Norwich, J: A History of Venice, Paperback, 18 June 1989

the Great Council. He stated: -

Trade is falling into final collapse. The ancient and long-held maxims and laws which created and could still create a state's greatness have been forgotten. We are supplanted by foreigners who penetrate right into the bowels of our city. We are despoiled of our substance, and not a shadow of our ancient merchants is to be found among our citizens or our subjects. Capital is lacking, not in the nation, but in commerce. It is used to support effeminacy, excessive extravagance, idle spectacles, pretentious amusements, and vice, instead of supporting and increasing industry, which is the mother of good morals, virtue, and of essential national trade.[377]

It was in this period of decline, in 1787, that **Francesco Foscolo (1739-1793),** son of Leonardo, from the San Stefano branch of the family, authored his famous Termination Report (*Pensionatico*), which concerned sheep grazing rights in Friuli. As trade began to wane, agricultural activities on the mainland became increasingly important to the Republic, as did grazing rights. Francesco was noted for his competence and intellect. He was a scholar, poet, and was by acclaim elected as honorary member of the public academy of agriculture, commerce, and arts of Verona. He was also a member of all the other agricultural academies of state. On his death in 1793, he was succeeded by his sons Marco and Leonardo. [378]

The members of the San Vio branch of the Foscolo family were the most active in the Great Council in the late 18th Century.

---

[377] Tabacco, G: Andrea Tron e la crisi dell'aristocrazia senatoria a Venezia, Trieste, Università degli Studi, 1957

[378] Cicogna, Emmanuele: Nelle Nozze Dell Nobile Daulo Augusto Di Foscolo Colla Baronessa Margh Degli Orefic,1842, Pp 10, 27

Georgio (Zozi) Foscolo (1761-1822), son of Daulo Augusto, was a Counsellor of the Civil Court of Venice and was also elected administrator of the Venetian Mint. In January 1789 he was elected a member of the Council of Forty and was an elector of Doge Ludivico Manin.[379] Manin descended from a family that had fled Florence and sought sanctuary in Friuli. Commanding vast wealth and landholdings on the mainland, the family was a brand-new house or casa novísima. Such houses were known colloquially as houses made for a penny, as nobility had been purchased. Manin's election stirred some controversy. The Patrician Pietro Gradenigo, who also served on the electing Council of Forty together with Foscolo famously exclaimed: - *I have made a Friulian Doge. The Republic is dead.*[380] As it turned out the Republics fortunes under Manin did not improve, and by 1792 the once great Venetian merchant fleet had declined to a mere 309 vessels.[381]

Two brothers of the afore mentioned Giorgio Foscolo, Marco and Francesco were also active in the Great Council at this time. **Marco Foscolo (1757-1817),** exercised civil offices in the magistracies of the Republic. He was elected to the Council of Forty hearing civil and criminal appeals, and later entered the priesthood. He was a well-respected member of the clergy, and in 1801 he was appointed Canon of Padua. He was a good Latinist and is credited for making significant contributions to the library of Padua. Marco was the first member of the Foscolo family to embrace an ecclesiastic career.[382] His brother **Francesco**

---

[379] Cicogna, Emmanuele: Nelle Nozze Dell Nobile Daulo Augusto Di Foscolo Colla Baronessa Margh Degli Orefic,1842, P 20
[380] Snow, C.P: The Two Cultures, Canto, 1993, p. 40.
[381] Anderson, R.C: Naval Wars in the Levant 1559-1853, Princton 1952
[382] ibid

Foscolo (1766-1826),[383] became a lawyer and was elected to the Council of Ten.

This brings us to 1797, when Napoleons troops entered Venice bringing an end to the Venetian Republic and nobility as it was known. A tumultuous period of change followed which brought a new concept of aristocracy for the two noble lines of the Foscolo family. This will be discussed in Chapter 3. However, before continuing with our examination of the two noble branches of the family, we pause to examine the genealogy of the great poet and Italian nationalist Ugo Foscolo, an important figure during the fall of the Republic.

Ionian Islands Sub-Branch of Poet Ugo Foscolo

It is well known the great poet Ugo Foscolo and his siblings lost their nobility, as generations of their family neglected to register marriages and births in the Venetian Golden Book. Giulio Constantino Angelo Foscolo, in a letter to his brother Ugo, reveals he was in love with a young woman of Hungarian nobility, but was unable to marry her as he did not have certified nobility.[384] Some genealogists wrongly suggest the lack of nobility is evidence that Ugo Foscolo descended from the medieval Candian branch of the family, with his ancestors moving to Corfu during the Candian Wars of the 17th Century. Some even go as far as to make tenuous and farfetched claims that Ugo Foscolo is descended from the Candian playwright Marco Antonio Foscolo. However, the evidence firmly establishes that the family of Ugo Foscolo

---

[383] Cicogna, Emmanuele: Nelle Nozze Dell Nobile Daulo Augusto Di Foscolo Colla Baronessa Margh Degli Orefic,1842, P 20

[384] Bibliotecaitaliana.it Archiviato il 16 settembre 2007 in Internet Archive, Lettera di Giulio ad Ugo del 3 agosto 1816

Republic of Venice

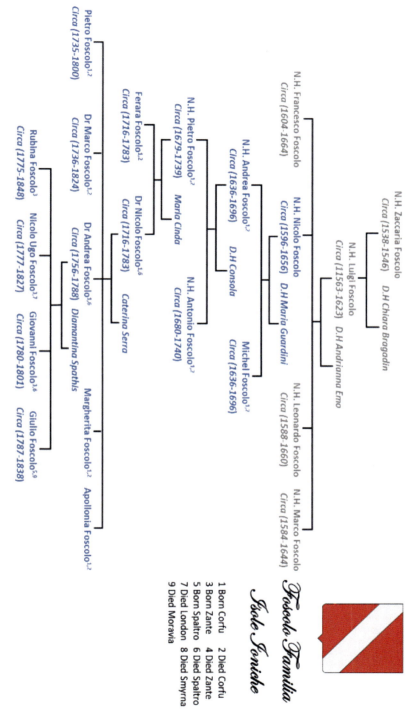

107

descended from the San Stefano branch of the family, from where hails the famous General Leonardo Foscolo (1588-1666). This is confirmed by Ugo Foscolo himself. In his last letter to Dionisio Chierico, written in London on the 15th of December 1826, he states: - *"documents from the Venetian archives prove my nobility, and my ancestry can be traced to the family of Genaral Leonardo Foscolo.*[385]

For convenience, we replicate the San Stefano sub-branch of the Foscolo family to which Ugo Foscolo belongs. Ugo Foscolo is shown to be descended from **Nicolò Foscolo (1596-1656)**, son of Luigi, and brother of the great General Leonardo Foscolo. The sub-branch progresses to **Andrea Foscolo (1636-1696)**, son of Nicolo, who was born in Corfu. From this time on, members of the sub-branch remain largely resident in the Ionian Islands. It is unknown from what point nobility was lost, but the break most likely occurred at a Pietro Foscolo (1679-1739), son of Andrea.

Although having lost their nobility, members of this sub-branch made significant contributions to the Republic. **Nicolò Foscolo (1716-1783),** son of Pietro, practiced medicine and moved to Spalatro in Dalmatia to administer the civil and military hospital.[386] His son **Andrea Foscolo (1756-1788),**[387] was likewise a doctor and trained in Padua. He had a reputation for being educated in the sciences, philosophy, and ancient languages. After completing his studies, he travelled to Zante, where he married Diamantina Spathia, widow of the Venetian noble Marco Serra. From this marriage Ugo Foscolo and his

---

[385] Foscolo, U; Sui Sepolcri Carme Di Ugo Foscolo, Lucca, coi tipi di Luigi Guidotti, 1844

[386] Gemelli, C: Della Vita E Opere Di Ugo Foscolo, Second Ed, Nicola Zanichelli, Bologna 1849

[387] ibid

siblings were born. Andrea, on the death of his father, moved to Spalatro, Dalmatia, where he took up his late father's post at the military hospital. It is known Ugo Foscolo attended Grammar School in Dalmatia. However, his father died at a young age, and Ugo Foscolo, his mother, and siblings eventually made their way back to Venice.[388]

---

[388] Gemelli, C: *Della Vita E Opere Di Ugo Foscolo*, Second Ed, Nicola Zanichelli, Bologna 1849

CHAPTER 3 POST REPUBLIC OF VENICE

The French Revolution and Napoleon Bonaparte's campaigns across Europe signalled a tumultuous time for Venetian Nobility. On 20 April 1792 France declared war against Prussia and Austria. Venice maintained a position of unarmed neutrality. However, on 1 May 1797 Napoleon declared war against Venice, and after only fifteen days Venice surrendered. Doge Luvidico Manin abdicated, and the Great Council met for the last time on 12 May 1797. A new democratic government was installed by the French, replacing the noble families who had governed the Republic exclusively since 1297. Many nobles fled to Austria. However, the new democratic state of Venice was short lived, with France and Austria signing the Treaty of Campoformio on 17 October 1797. As part of the treaty, Venice excluding the Ionian Islands, was handed to the Austrian Crown. Venice became a separate province of the Austrian Archduchy, with Francis I of Habsburg becoming the Duke of Venice. The province was governed by a Viennese Governor but maintained existing Venetian Legislation and currency. In 1805, as part of the Treaty of Pressburg, Venetian Territory was ceded to the Napoleonic Kingdom of Italy, and again in 1815 it returned to Austria by terms of the Final Act of the Congress of Vienna and became part of the Crown Land of Lombardy-Venetia.[389]

In the tumultuous period following the fall of the Republic, **Ugo Foscolo (1777-1827)**, son of Andrea, loomed large. Born in Zante (Zakynthos), Ugo was descended from the noble San Stefano branch of the family but was from a sub-branch which

---

[389] Lane, F: Venice, a maritime republic, Johns Hopkins U Press, 1973

had relocated to the Ionian Islands and had lost its nobility. His widowed mother settled in Venice in 1793 and struggled financially. However, young Ugo's love affair with widowed noblewoman, Isabella Teotochi Albrizzi, delivered him both financial security and an introduction into aristocratic circles. He completed his studies at the University of Padua, where he was influenced by Abbé Melchiore Cesarotti, a lecturer whose version of Ossian had gained great acclaim. His literary career began with the tragedy Tieste in 1797, which attracted modest success. Heavily involved in politics of the time he was a fervent supporter of Napoleon and the Jacobin movement, which he expected would overthrow the Venetian oligarchy. In poetry, he celebrated the freedoms proclaimed by the French Revolution in Ode A Bonaparte Liberatore, 1797. Hot headed and passionate he involved himself in activist causes, once leading a band of contemporaries in an affray intended to free Jews from a local ghetto.[390],[391]

On the fall of the Republic, he served on national committees in the short-lived democratic government of Venice. [392] The Campoformio Treaty which saw Napoleon hand Venice to the Austrians, saw Foscolo flee Venice for Milan. Despite this political development, Ugo Foscolo continued to maintain hope in Napoleon's pledge of a democratic Italy. Foscolo's state of mind is reflected in his widely acclaimed novel The Last Letters of Jacopo Ortis, 1798. The novel follows the mental sufferings and

---

[390] Chisholm, Hugh (ed.). Encyclopædia Britannica. 27 (11th ed.). Cambridge University Press. pp. 730–731.
[391] Gemelli, C: *Della Vita E Opere Di Ugo Foscolo*, Second Ed, Nicola Zanichelli, Bologna 1849
[392] ibid

Foscolo Family of Venice: Patricans and Aristocrats (A Genealogy)

Portrait of Ugo Foscolo, Francois-Xavier Fabre

Postage Stamp bearing Ugo Foscolos' Image

eventual suicide of an undeceived Italian patriot.[393]

On his arrival in Milan Ugo kept company with fellow poet Giuseppe Parini and befriended Italian Composer Vittorio Monti. He also gained a reputation as a serial womanizer. He took multiple lovers including Teresa Pikler, wife of his friend Vittorio Monti. Amongst other love interests were Isabella Roncioni, Antonietta Fagnani Arese, Marzia Martinengo, Maddalena Bignami, Quirina Mocenni Magiotti, and the English Lady Fanny Emerytt Hamilton.[394]

Whilst in Milan Foscolo's political activities became more intense and eventually in 1799, still hoping an independent Italy would be formed by Napoleon, he took up arms as a volunteer in the Cisalpine army (the Italian division of the French army). He fought against the Austro-Russians, taking part in the battle of the Trebbia and the siege of Genoa, where he was wounded and made prisoner.

It was not long after Foscolo return to Milan that Lady Hamilton announced her pregnancy.[395] His response to the news of impending fatherhood was to arrange an immediate posting to active service. He served as an officer in the Cisalpine in France from 1804 to 1806, preparing for an Invasion of England.[396] When released from the military he returned to Milan, and there completed his final edits to Jacopo Ortis, published a translation and commentary of Callimachus, worked on his version of the

---

[393] Gemelli, C: Della Vita E Opere Di Ugo Foscolo, Second Ed, Nicola Zanichelli, Bologna 1849
[394] ibid
[395] Vincent E.R.P: Ugo Foscolo: An Italian in Regency England, Cambridge, 1953
[396] Gemelli (n393)

Iliad, and began his translation of Laurence Sterne's Sentimental Journey. He also took part in a failed memorandum intended to present a new model of unified Italian government to Napoleon.[397] In 1807, Foscolo wrote his work Dei Sepolcri, and in 1809 he commenced a short and controversial tenure as chair of Italian eloquence at the University of Pavia. Discouraged by Napoleons failure to deliver freedom to Italians, in a lecture series Foscolo urged his young countrymen to study literature, "not in obedience to academic traditions, but in their relation to individual and national life and growth", a provocative move that stirred a populist movement for Italian nationalism. The sensation produced by the lecture provoked a decree from Napoleon himself, with the chair of national eloquence being abolished at all Italian universities. Soon afterwards, Foscolo released the tragedy Ajax, with little success because of its criticism of powerful people in the administration including Napoleon himself. Forced to leave Milan he moved to Florence in 1813, where he completed his version of Sentimental Journey. He returned to Milan later in 1813, until the entry of the Austrians when he was forced into exile. He first went to Switzerland, where he wrote a fierce satire in Latin on his political and literary opponents, and then in 1816 he moved to England.[398]

Ugo Foscolo was well received in England and lived an extravagant lifestyle from the large earnings he received from his literary work. In London Foscolo worked on his novel The Three Graces, and a translation of the Iliad. He took up accommodation at St Johns Wood, with three household staff. In his employ were two young maids, who were sisters, and whom Foscolo "guarded

---

[397] Gemelli, C: Della Vita E Opere Di Ugo Foscolo, Second Ed, Nicola Zanichelli, Bologna 1849
[398] ibid

Like a dragon." It turned out both these girls were prostitutes. When Foscolo's translator, American William G. Graham, became too intimate with one of the sisters, Foscolo took issue, and a duel was arranged. Fortunately, both shots missed, but when Graham returned to the St Johns Wood house to collect his belongings, Foscolo gave him a merciless beating with his fists.[399] Described by fellow poet Lord Byron as being as "Ugly as a baboon", Carolina Russell saw him in a completely different light. In one of her many love letters to Foscolo, she writes affectionately: - *Come and see me my little lothario, I will try to make you happy*.[400]

Soon his excesses led to financial problems, and he amounted significant debts. For reasons of belated paternal affection, or more likely access to a significant inheritance, he reunited with his daughter Floriana in 1822. They lived together in his final years. Wracked by ill health and the nagging of creditors, he died in the company of a few friends on 10 September 1827 and was buried in Chiswick Cemetery.[401]

Ugo Foscolo staunch resistance to Austrian rule was not shared by his younger brother **Giulio Constantine Angelo Foscolo (1787-1838)**. Around 1800 Giulio travelled from Venice to Milan where his brother Ugo Foscolo himself took charge of his education.[402] Later Giulio became a Cavalry officer in the Cisalpine, the Italian Division of Napoleons army, stationed in Vigevano. In 1811 he transferred to the Cisalpine Military Riding

---

[399] Vincent E.R.P: Ugo Foscolo: An Italian in Regency England, Cambridge, 1953
[400] ibid
[401] ibid
[402] Lettera di Foscolo alla madre del 3 febbraio 1809, Nelle Arrigioni, C; Il suicidio nei Foscolo. Torino, Edizioni l'Impronta 1951

School in Lodi, where in 1812 he was promoted to the rank of Captain. In 1813 Giulio advanced to become director of the Lodi Riding School.[403] It was shortly after this that Napoleon ceded the Lombardy region to the Austrian-Hungarian Empire, and General Bellegarde became the Viceroy of Lombardy on behalf of the Emperor of Austria. The Cisalpine was demobilized, and many officers were fired or transferred to peripheral regions of the Austrian-Hungarian Empire. However, Giulio made a very different choice from that of his brother Ugo. On 31 March 1815, he took an oath of loyalty to the Austrian Emperor and continued to serve as director of the Lodi Riding School, now as an officer in the Austro-Hungarian Army. It was at the riding school, where Giulio received a visit from General Bellegarde himself, the Viceroy.[404] At their meeting Giulio was asked to convince his brother Ugo to abandon his anti-Austrian convictions. Despite Giulios best efforts and close relationship with his brother, it proved unsuccessful, and on 6 October 1815 he was transferred to Hungary where he was stationed at a remote facility one day away from Buda and Pest, three days from Presburg, and four days from Vienna.[405] The conditions were harsh, and in March 1816 Giulio asked for medical leave, which was granted. From 1818 to 1822 Giulio was back in Hungary with the post of cavalry squad commander. In 1822 he was ordered to Vienna, where his Squad was reviewed by The Emperor himself. Impressed with Giulio's Equestrian skills, he remained in Vienna for several months, as an equestrian instructor.[406] However, by August of the same year, Giulio was posted to Blanitz in Moravia where in 1830 he was

---

403 Arrigioni, C; *Il suicidio nei Foscolo. Torino*, Edizioni l'Impronta 1951
404 Lettera di Giulio ad Ugo del 10 dicembre 1815, Nelle Arrigioni, C; *Il suicidio nei Foscolo. Torino*, Edizioni l'Impronta 1951
405 ibid
406 ibid

promoted to the rank of Major, and then in 1832 to Lieutenant Colonel.[407] In 1836 Giulio moved back to Hungary where his health deteriorated and where in 1837, he committed suicide.[408]

The Kingdom of Lombardy-Venezia

The Kingdom of Lombardy-Venezia was formed by the Final Act of the Congress of Vienna in 1815 and was ruled by the respective Austrian Emperors as King. The King was represented day to day by the Viceroy (in later years a Governor General), which was appointed by the Court in Vienna and who was resident in Milan and Venice.

In accordance with prevailing Austrian-Hungary laws at the time, any noble living in Habsburg ruled lands, who owed their allegiance to the dynasty and therefore The Emperor, were considered part of the Austrian Aristocracy. Those Venetian nobles registered in the Golden Book at the fall of Venice in 1797, were eligible to acquire Austrian nobility. The eligible Foscolo family members were conferred Austrian Nobility by Sovereign Resolution in the early 19th Century, as shown In the Table. Nobility was no longer based on registration in the Golden Book, but once conferred followed agnatic-cognatic succession as prescribed by Austria-Hungarian law. Succession was reserved for male descendants by order of birth (primogeniture), but in the event of extinction of the male line, title would pass to female members based on order of birth.

Although the Kingdom of Lombardy-Venetia was administered in the Italian language, it was plagued by instability created by the

---

[407] Arrigioni, C; Il suicidio nei Foscolo. Torino, Edizioni l'Impronta 1951
[408] ibid

Foscolo Family of Venice: Patricans and Aristocrats (A Genealogy)

Name	Branch	Conferred Nobility
Alessandro Foscolo *of Daulo Augusto*	San Vio	Sovereign Resolution 11 November 1817
Marco Foscolo *of Daulo Augusto*	San Vio	Sovereign Resolution 11 November 1817
Francesco Foscolo *of Daulo Augusto*	San Vio	Sovereign Resolution 16 November 1817
Leonardo Foscolo *of Daulo Augusto*	San Vio	Sovereign Resolution 11 November 1817
Giorgio Foscolo *of Daulo Augusto*	San Vio	Sovereign Resolution 28 December 1818
Marco Foscolo *of Francesco*	San Stefano	Sovereign Resolution 28 April 1821
Leonardo Foscolo *of Francesco*	San Stefano	Sovereign Resolution 28 April 1821

Members of the Foscolo family conferred Austrian nobility in Kingdom of Lombardy - Venezia

Italian Unification Movement (*Risorgiomento*). Austrians mistrusted and refused the local aristocrats from high government offices, as they traditionally had rejected university education and had gained leadership positions purely through family background. Deprived of careers in the administration, many Patricians left Venice, while others actively supported the wars of independence against the Austrians.[409]

The San Vio Branch remained largely in Venice. **Giovanni Battista Foscolo (1791–1851)**, son of Giorgio, was appointed a Lieutenant in the Austrian-Hungarian Navy and worked as a Chamberlin for the new administration[410]. His brother, **Daulo August Foscolo (1785-1860)** took up an ecclesiastic career and was ordained in the Cathedral of San Marco in Venice in 1808. He was appointed an Archbishop on 8 March 1816 by Pope Pius VII and became Archbishop of Corfu on 17 October 1816. He returned to Venice and in 1830 he was appointed by Pope Pius VIII to the honorific post of Patriarch of Jerusalem, and in 1847 to the honorific post of Patriarch of Alexandria. As these were both honorific posts, he continued to reside in Venice until his death.[411]

Social discourse eventually led to a rebellion in 1848, backed by Sardinian troops. This led briefly to the declaration of a Lombardy provisional Government. The rebellion was put down in a matter of months and Austrian rule restored.

---

[409] Schönhals, K: Erinnerungen eines österreichischen Veteranen aus dem italienischen Kriege der Jahre 1848 und 1849

[410] Schroder, F, Repertorio Genealogico Delle Famiglie Confermate Nobili e Dei Titolati Nobili, Venice, 1830

[411] ibid

Foscolo Family of Venice: Patricans and Aristocrats (A Genealogy)

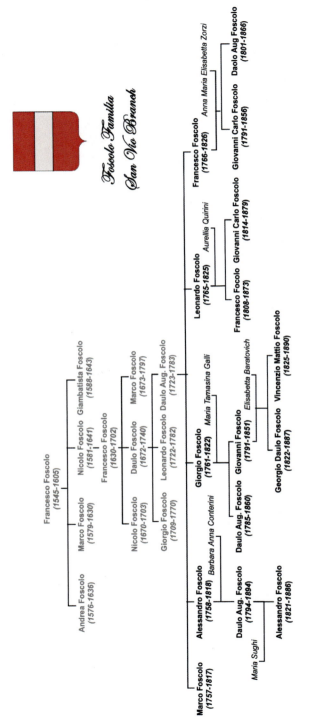

The Kingdom of Italy

The Austrians were finally defeated in the second Italian War of Independence in 1859. The Treaty of Zurich ceded Lombardy to the French Emperor Napoleon III who immediately ceded the territory to the Kingdom of Sardinia (the embryonic Kingdom of Italy). Most of the states of the peninsula together with the Kingdom of the Two Sicily's were united under King Victor Emmanuel II of the Savoy dynasty, who up until this time had been the monarch of the Kingdom of Sardinia, which included Piedmont. Venice and Mantua were ceded to the Kingdom of Italy in 1866. Rome itself remained under the Papacy until 1870, after which it also became part of the Kingdom of Italy.[412]

Under the unified Kingdom of Italy, there was an attempt to impose a uniform nobility law. As part of this, all-male descendants of Venetian nobility inscribed in the Golden Book at the end of the Republic in 1797, together with those who were conferred Austrian nobility, received Italian titles. Members of the Foscolo family from the surviving two noble branches, received the title of Count (*Conte*) with no territorial designation. Succession changed to Salic law. This restricted the pool of potential heirs to males on order of birth (primogeniture). Females were totally excluded from succession. However, the loss of nobility became less of an issue relative to the Republic, as the only requirement for succession was a male heir.

For the most part the San Vio Branch of the Foscolo family remained in Italy, where descendants remain to the present day. The San Stefano Branch developed into two sub-branches, one

---

[412] Smith, D.M:Moderen Italy: A Political History, University of Michigan Press, 1997

that remained in Italy, the second established itself in the Levant. As the latter is the least documented of the two sub-branches we will consider it in greater detail in the next chapter, Chapter 4.

CHAPTER 4 LEVANT SUB-BRANCH

The San Stefano branch of the Foscolo family, although arguably containing some of the most historically significant figures, has not been well documented. The reasons for this are threefold. First, the most famous figure in the branch, General Leonardo Foscolo, died childless. Second, of the two remaining San Stefano sub-branches, the one containing the famous poet Ugo Foscolo, relocated to the Ionian Islands losing its nobility. Third, the only remaining San Stefano sub-branch was forced to repair its nobility in the 18th Century, due to a marriage that occurred outside the Republic. The famous genealogist and writer Emmanuele Cicogna confirmed the existence of the San Stefano branch of the Foscolo family. He suggested the investigation of the marriage between Leonardo Foscolo and Elena Stratti in 1738 delayed their offspring's entry into the Golden Book, giving the impression that the sub-branch had lost nobility.

The lesser-known San Stefano branch contained only two members at the end of the Venetian Republic, Leonardo Foscolo, son of Fancesco, and his brother Marco. Marco Foscolo and his descendants remained in Italy until the present day. Leonardo Foscolo moved to the Levant in the early 19th Century, where the branched flourished. This section will focus on this less documented Levant sub-branch.

Life in the Levant

Sometime after the fall of the Republic, **Leonardo Foscolo (1765-1829)** relocated from Venice to Smyrna, Ottoman Empire (Modern day Izmir, Turkey). Smyrna was a thriving trading hub at the time, and Leonardo established himself as a merchant. The

Foscolo Family of Venice: Patricans and Aristocrats (A Genealogy)

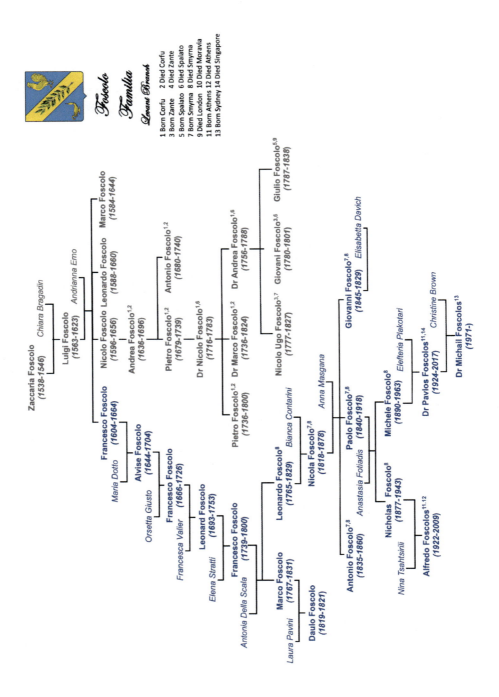

Foscolo the family lived in the fashionable Trasser district of the city.

Nicolo Foscolo (1818-1878), [413] Son of the afore mention Leonardo, married Anna Masgana, the granddaughter of the first doctor appointed to the National Hospital in Smyrna. They had three sons, Antonio, Giovanni, and Paulo. Nicolo together with his eldest son Antonio established the Foscolo-Mango Steamship Company in Constantinople (Istanbul, Turkey). Their partner was Anthony Mango an Italian from the Island of Chios. The Company enjoyed success in the late 19th Century, until its demise during the great depression in 1929. Antonio Foscolo died young without male heirs. **Giovanni Foscolo (1739-1800)** the younger son of Nicolo married Elisabetta Davich and had two daughters Malvina and Angela. He worked for the family businesses in Smyrna. **Paolo Foscolo (1840-1918)**, [414] the middle son and heir of Nicolo, inherited a large estate in Seydiköy south of Smyrna from his maternal uncle. Maintaining a house in Smyrna as the family's residence in the coldest winter months, the family moved to the magnificent mansion at Seydiköy. Paulo married Anna Fotiadis, daughter of Ioannis. The Fotiadis family was arguably the wealthiest and one of the most influential in the local area. The family had origins from the Peloponnese. They became rich with Anastasios, brother of Ioannis, who had emigrated to Egypt and gained the sympathy of a Pasha. Anastasios, with the influence of the Pasha, was able to corner the Egyptian cotton market. The family then settled in Seydiköy and built a mansion with 40 rooms, very extensive gardens, and -

---

413 Karas, N: Seydiköy the Levent town of Smyrna, a history of life, Tsevdo, Athens, 1964
414 ibid

Fotiadis family Mansion, Seydiköy

Rail Service funded by the Fotiadis family.

vineyards. The Fotiadis family financed the railway junction between Seydiköy and Smyrna, which offered 5 daily services. It was bought 20 years after its construction (in 1908) by British Aydın Railways. Paulo Foscolo had two sons, Nicholas Foscolo and Michele Foscolo and two daughters Eleni Foscolo and Aglaia Foscolo. Eleni Foscolo died when she was 17 years of age.[415]

Seydiköy (modern day Gaziemir, Turkey) was known as a cosmopolitan town 16 km South of Smyrna, about 40 minutes by train. It had a population of 6,276 in 1824 and was the summer residence of many affluent Europeans working in Smyrna. Jacob Van Dam, Consul of Holland in Smyrna from 1668 to 1688, had a house in Seydiköy. British Consul in Smyrna and Botanist, William Sherard, also lived in Seydiköy in the 1700's. George van Lennep, chief merchant of the Dutch trade station and Dutch Consul in Smyrna, settled his family in Seydiköy in 1731. The van Lennep's were prominent traders and landowners with 3900 acres of tobacco plantations at Malcajik (now Bulgurca) 13 km south of Seydiköy. Later in 1760's another aristocratic Dutch family settled in Seydiköy, the family of Hungarian Count Daniel de Hochepieds, Consul of Holland in Smyrna at the time. Baron van Heemstra also owned a farm in the nearby village of Oğlanesi. It follows the town of Seydiköy was much more than an outpost.[416]

The Foscolo estate in Seydiköy was originally owned by a Dutchman, Wilkmann, who sold it to Michael Masgana, the maternal uncle of Paolo Foscolo. The property was extensive, 741 acres, making Foscolo one of the largest landowners in Seydiköy.

---

[415] Karas, N: Seydiköy the Levent town of Smyrna, a history of life, Tsevdo, Athens, 1964
[416] ibid

The estate began in the township and extended to the outlying mountainous area. The property had olive groves, 37 acres of vineyards, pistachio trees, fig trees, myrtles and a large pond containing eels and fish. A winding road led to a spring with fountain, surrounded by plane trees, and a mountain forested by pine trees. Paulo Foscolo allowed all inhabitants of the township, as well as their guests from Smyrna, free access to his lands. They came for nature walks, and sometimes in the summer, on Sunday or other days of celebration, they picnicked at the spring known as the Plane Tree of Foscolo, where they spent their day by the cool waters shaded by trees. Inside the estate there were private residences of the household staff including the Director of the Estate, and the Overseer. The estate was a working estate and there were stables, warehouses, and stock yards. In addition to fresh produce, the estate also commercially produced olive oil, red wines and ports, cognac, and liqueurs, employing specialist distillers and wine makers. At the entrance of the estate stood the Foscolo mansion with over 40 rooms, and its many reception halls. The mansion was surrounded by a large garden containing a rotunda, multiple flower beds, and rose beds with many rare varieties of roses. Many festivities and dances were held at the estate.[417]

A major event was held at the Foscolo estate just before World War I, in 1914, when the pride of the Austro-Hungarian Navy SMS Tegetthoff and her sister ship SMS Viribus Unitis, together with SMS Zrínyi, and SMS Monarch, called at the port of Smyrna under the command of Vice-Admiral Maximilian Njegovan. The Vice-admiral and the officers of the Austrian fleet were guests of

---

[417] Karas, N: Seydiköy the Levent town of Smyrna, a history of life, Tsevdo, Athens, 1964

Vice-Admiral Maximilian Njegovan

Austrian Fleet in Smyrna

Foscolo Family of Venice: Patricans and Aristocrats (A Genealogy)

Paolo Foscolo

Paulo Foscolo Mansion, Seydköy

Garden party at Paulo Foscolo Mansion, Seydköy, Michele Foscolo second from right bottom

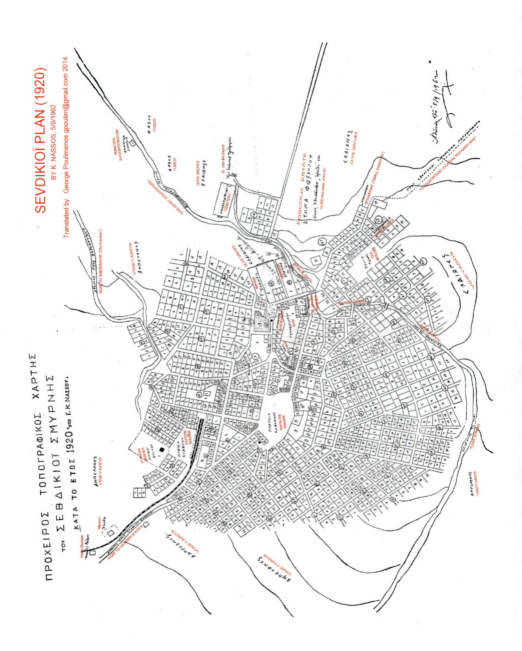

***Map of the Seydiköy showing Foscolo family estate,
Source*: Karas (1964)**

Paolo Foscolo at his Seydiköy estate. Although the Foscolo family, were from 1866 Ciitizens of the Kingdom of Italy, and Paolo Foscolo now held the Italian title of Count (Conte) without territory, it is worth remembering at the time Paulo Foscolo through his father Nicolo, additionally held aristocratic title of Count (*Graf*) bestowed by the Austrian-Hungarian Emperor. Many dignitaries, and members of Smyrna's high society gathered at the estate for the function and dined on the magnificent buffet catered by two of the largest patisseries in Smyrna, Kafe Kosti and High Life Cafe. [418]

The 1922 Greek-Turkish Wars

The Levant Sub-branch of the Foscolo family did not participate in World War I. However, developments following the war would bring an idyllic existence to a dramatic end.

On 30 October 1918, the Armistice of Mudros was signed between the Ottoman Empire and the Entente Powers (Great Britain, Greece, Italy, France, and the United States). This ended the Ottoman front of World War I. The Entente Powers then began to discuss the partition of Ottoman territories. These negotiations began in February 1919 and each country had distinct negotiating preferences about Smyrna. The French, who had large investments in the region, supported a Turkish state that would include the zone of Smyrna. The Italian position was that Smyrna was rightfully their possession.[419] Greece, represented by Greek Prime Minister Venizelos supported what was referred to as

---

[418] Karas, N: Seydiköy the Levent town of Smyrna, a history of life, Tsevdo, Athens, 1964

[419] Llewellyn-Smith, M: Ionian Vision: Greece in Asia Minor, 1919–1922, (New edition, 2nd impression ed.). London: C. Hurst. 1998 p. 92

Megali, which advocated bringing areas with a majority Greek population or with historical and religious ties to Greece under control of the Greek state. The Greek position was supported by Britains Lloyd George, who began a large propaganda effort to promote their claim to Smyrna[420] Moreover, the Greek claim over the Smyrna area, which appeared to have a clear Greek majority, were supported by Woodrow Wilson's Fourteen Points which emphasized the right to autonomous development for minorities in Anatolia. [421] Despite French and Italian objections, by the middle of February 1919 Lloyd George shifted the discussion to how Greek administration would work, and not whether Greek administration would happen.[422] In late February 1919, Venezilos appointed Aristeidis Stergiadis the High Commissioner of Smyrna. In April 1919, the Italians landed and took over Antalya and began showing signs of moving troops towards Smyrna.[423] Lloyd George saw an opportunity to break the impasse over Smyrna and concocted a report that an armed uprising of Turkish guerrillas in the Smyrna area was seriously endangering the Greek and other Christian minorities. [424] Both to protect local Christians and also to limit increasing Italian action in Anatolia, French Prime Minister Georges Clemenceau and U.S. President Woodrow Wilson supported a Greek military occupation of Smyrna.[425] Although Smyrna would be occupied by Greek troops,

---

420 Llewellyn-Smith, M: Ionian Vision: Greece in Asia Minor, 1919–1922, (New edition, 2nd impression ed.). London: C. Hurst. 1998 p. 92
421 Turkish General Staff, Türk İstiklal Harbinde Batı Cephesi, Edition II, Part 2, Ankara 1999, p. 225
422 Montgomery, A. E: The Making of the Treaty of Sèvres of 10 August 1920. The Historical Journal. 15 (4), 1972, pp775–787.
423 Jensen, P. K: The Greco-Turkish War, 1920–1922. International Journal of Middle East Studies, 10 (4), 1979, pp 553–565.
424 ibid
425 ibid

authorized by the Allies, the Allies did not agree that Greece would take sovereignty over the territory until further negotiations settled this issue. [426] The Greek occupation was authorized following the Treaty of Sèvres (1920).

Following an overthrow of the Greek Government in which Eleftherios Venizelos was replaced by and absolute monarchy under King Constantine of Greece, the allies withdrew their support for the Greek army. This left the Greek troops in Smyrna without money and arms. Rather than retreat, the King pushed on further into Anatolia and took control of the western and north-western part of Anatolia, including the cities of Manisa, Balıkesir, Aydın, Kütahya, Bursa and Eskişehir. However, Mustafa Kemal atta Turk reorganized what was a growing Nationalist movement into a strong Turkish army, and the Greek Army's advance was checked by Turkish forces at the Battle of Sakarya in 1921. The Greek front collapsed with the Turkish counterattack in August 1922, and the Greek troops began to withdraw.[427]

As the last Greek troops evacuated Smyrna on the evening of Friday 8 September 1922, the first elements of Mustafa Kemal's forces, a Turkish cavalry squadron, made its way into the city. At the outset, the Turkish occupation of the city was orderly. The inhabitants reasoned that the presence of an allied fleet would discourage any violence against the Christian community. On the morning of 9 September 1922, no fewer than 21 Allied warships lay at anchor in Smyrna's harbour. As a precaution, sailors and marines from the allied fleet were landed ashore to guard their

---

[426] Jensen, P. K: The Greco-Turkish War, 1920–1922. International Journal of Middle East Studies, 10 (4), 1979, pp 553–565.
[427] ibid

respective diplomatic compounds. However, they were given strict orders to maintain neutrality if violence broke out between the Turks and the Christians.[428]

As Turkish troops secured the city, order and discipline began to break down among the Turkish troops, who began systematically targeting the Armenian population, pillaging their shops, looting their homes, separating the men from the women and sexually assaulting the latter.[429] The Greek Orthodox Metropolitan Bishop, Chrysostomos, was tortured and hacked to death by a Turkish mob in full view of French soldiers, who were prevented from intervening by their commanding officer.[430] Refuge by the civilian population was sought in the American and the European quarters. The desperate victims were strenuously turned away by foreign missions, so as not to antagonize or harm relations with the leaders of the Turkish Nationalist movement. A large hotel which had Greek guests was set on fire, and the Turks then placed a machine gun opposite the entrance and opened fire as guests tried to escape the blaze.[431] Victims of the massacres committed by the Turkish army and irregulars were also foreign citizens. Dutch merchant Oscar de Jongh and his wife were murdered by the Turkish cavalry,[432] while in another incident a retired British doctor was beaten to death in his home trying to prevent the rape

---

[428] Dobkin, M.H.: Smyrna 1922: The Destruction of a City, 1971; 2nd ed. Kent, Ohio: Kent State University Press, 1988.
[429] ibid, pp. 120–167.
[430] Ibid, pp. 133–134.
[431] Schaller D. J., Zimmerer J: Late Ottoman Genocides – Schaller: The Dissolution of the Ottoman Empire and Young Turkish Population and Extermination Policies. Routledge, 2013, p. 46.
[432] ibid

Greek troops withdrawing from Smyrna.

Smyrna a blaze as seen from an Italian Naval Cruiser

of a servant girl.[433] The city was set ablaze by Turkish troops. Many civilians who succeeded in reaching Smyrna harbour drowned in their attempt to escape. The fortunate were finally evacuated by Greek, Italian, and American ships.

The Foscolo family was not untouched by events. Their Trasser house was destroyed in the great fire of Smyrna, and many possessions lost. As Italian Citizens and aristocrats the family was spared from harm at the hands of the Turkish Nationalists, and it did not go unrecorded that members of the Foscolo family used their immunity to help many victims of these horrific events escape death. [434]

Tensions were running high and as the Foscolo family were known to have adopted many aspects of Hellenic culture by that time, they feared becoming victims themselves. The family decided to abandon the bulk of their possessions and property and flee the region together with other foreign nationals. The family were evacuated on an Italian naval cruiser in late 1922, with the intention of repatriating to Venice. However, things took a turn when a heated argument erupted between Michele Foscolo and the Captain of the vessel over the treatment of Greek refugees. In Smyrna harbour the captain had ordered his crew to pour boiling oil over the side of the vessel, to prevent fleeing Greeks from boarding. In protest, and disgust, he and his brother Nicholas together with their sister Aglaia disembarked in Athens, Greece.

The Foscolo family bought homes in the then upper middle-class

---

[433] Murat, J: The Great Extirpation of Hellenism and Christianity in Asia Minor: The Historic and Systematic Deception of World Opinion

[434] Jensen, P. K: The Greco-Turkish War, 1920–1922. International Journal of Middle East Studies, 10 (4), 1979, pp 553–565.

suburb of Kypseli, Athens. Aglaia Foscolo married a Greek Civil Engineer Simopoulous and had one daughter Anastasia. **Nicholas Foscolo (1890-1963)** used his connections to secure work in public administration. He married Nina Tsahtsirili of Seydiköy and had one son Alfredo and two daughters Eleni and Anastasia. **Alfredo Foscolos (1920-2009)** gained a degree in Political Science from the Panteion School of Political Science, Athens and worked in public administration. He remained unmarried with no children. **Michele Foscolo (1890-1963)** was fluent in Italian, French, Greek, Turkish, and held a degree in Commerce from the University of Florence. He was able to secure employment as a specialist banker and began work at the Bank of Anatolia in Athens, which was later absorbed by the National Bank of Greece. He was married to Elefteria Plakotaris of Seydiköy and produced two children Pavlos Foscolos and Anastasia Foscolos. **Dr Pavlos Foscolos (1924-2017)**, son of Michele, took up arms in the resistance movement during World War II. He later graduated with a medical degree from the University of Athens, specializing in Gynaecology and Obstetrics under the supervision of Professor Louros. His thesis "placenta previa" was well received and gained acclaim at the international level. After spending thirteen years in the Hellenic Airforce as a medical officer, he was discharged with the rank of Wing Commander. He emigrated to Australia in 1959, where he served the Greek community in Sydney first as a Gynaecologist and Obstetrician, and in his later years as a General Practitioner. He retired to Singapore at age 81. He married Christine Brown, a British National, and had one son Dr Michail Foscolos. **Dr Michail Foscolos (1971)** graduated in Engineering and Law from the University of New South Wales, Sydney, and completed a Doctorate in Economics and Finance at Imperial College, University of London. His thesis in the field of Artificial

Intelligence in Finance completed in 1993 gained international acclaim and was published at the international level. He was an academic for a time, serving as a Professor of Banking and Finance. He then moved to financial services where he worked for over 20 years. In the 1990s he served on the Australian Stock Exchange Index Advisory panel that gave rise to the ASX Stock Market indices used in Australia to this day. He advised Australian Government on finance related matters in the 1990s, and in the 2000s served as an Investment Consultant to Southeast Asian pension and national funds with over US$400 Billion under his advice. He served as Chief Executive Officer of US$7 Billion Hedge fund before serving in senior banking roles in the Wealth Management space in 2010s.

CHAPTER 5 TITLES AND HERALDRY

Titles

In the Venetian Republic 1265 to 1797, members of the two noble branches of the Foscolo family, held the title Patrizio Veneto. The title was abbreviated to the prenominal "NH" (Nobilis Homo) for men, and "ND" (Nobilis Donna) for women. Holding the title of a Venetian Patrician was a great honour and many European Kings and Princes, as well as foreign noble families, were known to have asked for this prestigious title.

In the Patriciate there was absolute political equality amongst members. Each vote, including that of the Doge (head of state), had the same value when electing officeholders. Every Patrician, in theory, had the same possibility of accessing public office or even being elected as Doge. A reflection of this principle was the equal title of "Nobleman" (Nobilis Homo) bestowed on all Patricians, without any distinction. Whoever held the title carried a portion of sovereignty in which every Patrician was a participant. Venetian Patricians were Princes of the Blood, each with the equal possibility of rising to the royal rank of Doge. Venetian Nobility and titles were extinguished in a decree by Doge Ludovico Manin just before his abdication in 1797 at the fall of the Venetian Republic.

Following the creation of the Kingdom of Lombardy-Venezia, members of the Foscolo family, who were inscribed in the Golden Book in 1797, and who swore allegiance to The Emperor of Austria, were conferred Austrian aristocratic title. The hereditary title conferred was that of Count (*Graf*), with female spouse styled Countess (*Grafin*). This title continues to this day through agnatic-cognatic succession.

In 1866 the newly formed Kingdom of Italy bestowed male descendants of those inscribed in the Golden Book in 1797, as well as those conferred Austrian nobility during the Kingdom of Lombardy-Venezia, Italian hereditary title of Count with no territorial designation. In addition to their Austrian title, male members of the two aristocratic lines of the Foscolo family were from 1866 styled Count (*Conte*), and female spouses were styled Countess (*Contessa*). The Italian title continues to this day through salic succession.

Following the collapse of the Austrian Empire in the aftermath of World War I, the Austrian Arbitration Act, 3 April 1919 (law on the Abolition of Nobility), abolished nobility, all noble privileges, and titles in Austria. Outside Austria use of these noble titles continued. In 1946, the Kingdom of Italy was replaced by a republic. Under the Italian Constitution adopted in 1948, titles of nobility are no longer legally recognized. However, they are not prohibited, and can still be used as a courtesy. For the Foscolo aristocratic lines where succession does not fail, both Austrian and Italian titles continue until this day as a courtesy.

Heraldry

Blazon of the Foscolo Family

The blazon was used by each the Frari branch, San Vio Branch, and San Stefano branch.

Heraldic Description

Gules a fesse argent

Fascia di argento su rosso

Blazon of San Stefano Branch, Ionian Islands Sub-Branch

The blazon was adopted by Andrea Foscolo (1636-1697), San Stefano Branch, and his descendants.

Heraldic Description

Gules a bend argent

banda di argento su rosso

Blazon San Stefano Branch, Levant Sub-Branch (1750-1866)

The blazon was adopted by Francisco Foscolo (1739-1800), San Stefano branch, and his descendants.

Heraldic Description

Azure, a bend or bearing laurel branch vert, in chief a rooster or, in base a lighted lamp of same.

amo di alloro di verde su banda di oro su azzurro accompagnata da in alto a destra un gallo di oro crestato di rosso e in basso a sinistra da una lampada

Coat of Arms of Count Foscolo, Levant Sub-Branch (From ca 1870).

Coat of arms used by all incumbent Conte di Foscolo of the San Stefano Levant sub-branch.

Heraldic Description

Azure a bend or, bearing laurel branch vert, and in chief a rooster or, in base a lighted lamp of same. Mantling Azure and or, forward helmet with coronet (Conte).

REFERENCES

Abulafia, D: *The Great Sea: A Human History of the Mediterranean*, Penguin, 2012
Alvise Zorzi, La République du Lion, Histoire de Venise
Anderson, R.C: Naval Wars in the Levant 1559-1853, Princton 1952
Anticanto, S: Frammenti Istorici Della Guerra in Dalmazia, Venezia, 1649
Armstrong, L and Kirshner, L: The Politics of Law in Late Medievalmand Renaissance Italy, U Toronto Press, 2011
Arrighi, G: The Long Twentieth Century, Verso, 1994
Arrigioni, C; Il suicidio nei Foscolo. Torino, Edizioni l'Impronta 1951
AvC, Raspe, Record, 3647, Folio 87r, 1417
Balard, M: Dal trattato di Milano al 1345. La lotta contro Genova, stituto dell'Enciclopedia Italiana, 2021
Bibliotecaitaliana.it Archiviato il 16 settembre 2007 in Internet Archive, Lettera di Giulio ad Ugo del 3 agosto 1816
Billanovich, G. & Chiara, M: CARRARA, Francesco da, il Novello, Dizionario Biografico degli Italiani, Vol 20: Carducci Carusi, Rome: Istituto dell Enciclopedia Italiana, 1977
Brill, E.J: First Encyclopaedia of Islam: 1913-1936, Vol 3, Leiden, New York, 1993
Calimani, R., Sullam, A, and Calimani D: The Venetian Ghetto, Mondadori, 2007 pp. 12, 90
Cappellari nel Campidoglio Veneto Codice MSS della Marciana
Cappellari; Reggimenti, Il mss
Cavaccia, G: Aula Zabarella Hugo Fuscus Familiae Fusculae originem dedisse agunt, typis J. de Cadorinis, 1670
Chasiotis, I: History of the Greek Nation, Volume XI: Hellenism under Foreign Rule (Period 1669 - 1821), Ekdotiki Athinon, 1975

Chisholm, Hugh (ed.). Encyclopædia Britannica. 27 (11th ed.). Cambridge University Press

Chojnacki, S: La formazione della nobiltà dopo la Serrata, in Storia di Venezia, Vol. 3, Treccani, 1997

Cicogna, E: Nelle Nozze Dell Nobile Daulo Augusto Di Foscolo Colla Baronessa Margh Degli Orefic, 1842

Consiglio dei Dieci, Mis, Register 6, folio 123r, 1373

Consiglio dei Dieci, Misti, Register 8, Folio 148r, Folio 87r.

Cook, M. A: Cambridge History of Islam and the New Cambridge Modern History, Cambridge University Press, 1976

Corano, A; Storia di Candia, Creta Sacra ii, MSS

Crescenzi, V: Stern Laura Ikins review of Esse de maiori consilio: Leggittimita civile e legittimazione politica nella repubblica di Venezia (secc. XIII-XVI), The American Journal of Legal History XLII, 1998

Dandalo R. I. S. tom xii

Davis, R.C and Ravid, B: The Jews of Early Modern Venice, John Hopkins University Press, 2001

Diehl, C: La Repubblica di Venezia, Newton & Compton editori, Roma, 2004

Dobkin, M.H.: Smyrna 1922: The Destruction of a City, 1971; 2nd ed. Kent, Ohio: Kent State University Press, 1988

Edbury, P: The Kingdom of Cyprus and the Crusades 1191–1374, Cambridge University Press, 1994

Enrica, A & Bongi, P: Sulle terre dei da Camino, Pieve da Soligo:Bubola & Naibo, 1993

Fabris, A: From Adrianople to Constantinople: Venetian–Ottoman diplomatic missions, 1360–1453, Mediterranean Historical Review, 7 (2), 1992

Faroqhi, S: The Ottoman Empire and the World Around It, I.B. Tauris, 2006

Finlay, G: The History of Greece under Othoman and Venetian Domination, William Blackwood and Sons, London, 185Finkel, C: Osman's Dream: The Story of the Ottoman Empire 1300–1923, John Murray, London, 2006

Fitzsimons, A. K: The political, Economic and Military Decline of Venice leading up to 1797, Thesis, University of North Texas, 2013

Flaminio Conaro: Ecces Ven, vi, xi, xiv

Foscolo, U: Sui Sepolcri Carme Di Ugo Foscolo, Lucca, coi tipi di Luigi Guidotti, 1844

Garnier, E: L'Alliance Impie, Editions du Felin, 2008

Galliciolli, II

Gemelli, C: Della Vita E Opere Di Ugo Foscolo, Second Ed, Nicola Zanichelli, Bologna, 1849

Graziani, Historia Veneta, II

Guérard, A: France: A Modern History, University of Michigan, 1959

Guilmartin, J. F: Galleons and Galleys: Gunpowder and the Changing Face of Warfare at Sea 1300–1650, Cassell, 2003

Gullino, G; Andrea Foscolo, Dizionario Biografico degli Italiani, Vol 49, 1997

Hrabak, B: Turske provale i osvajanja na području današnje severne Dalmacije do sredine XVI. Stoleća, Journal Institute of Croatian History, University of Zagreb, 1986

Hazlitt, W. C: The Venetian Republic: Its Rise. Its Growth, and Its Fall 421-1797 Nabu (first published 1900), 2011

Hope, C: Chroniques Greco-Romanes, Avec Notes et Tables Genealogiques, Berlin, 1873 Inscriz Veneziane, Vol iv

Iordanou, I: The Spy Chiefs of Renaissance Venice: Intelligence Leadership in the Early Modern World, Spy Chiefs, Volume 2, Intelligence Leaders in Europe, the Middle East, and Asia, Georgetown U Press, 2018

Jensen, P. K: The Greco-Turkish War, 1920–1922. International Journal of Middle East Studies, 10 (4), 1979

Karas, N: Seydiköy the Levent town of Smyrna, a history of life, Tsevdo, Athens, 1964

Kiesewetter, A: LADISLAO d'Angiò Durazzo, re di Sicilia. Dizionario Enciclopedico degli Italiani, Enciclopedia Italiana, 2011

Konstantinidou, K, Mantadakis E, Falaga M, Sardi, T, and Samonis, G: Venetian Rule and Control of Plague Epidemics on the Ionian Islands during 17th and 18th Centuries, Emerg Infect Dis,15(1), 2009.

Lane,F: Venice and History:The Collected Papers of Frederic C. Lane, Baltimore, The Johns Hopkins Press, 1966

Lane, F: Venice, a maritime republic. Johns Hopkins University Press, 1973

Lewis, B, Pellat, C. & Schacht, J: The Encyclopaedia of Islam, New Edition, Volume II, 1965

Lewis, B: The Central Islamic Lands from Pre-Islamic Times to the First World War, Cambridge University Press, 1978

Llewellyn-Smith, M: Ionian Vision: Greece in Asia Minor, 1919–1922, (New edition, 2nd impression ed.). London: C. Hurst. 1998

Locatelli, Storia della Guerra in Levante, II

Luttrel, A: The Latins of Argos and Nauplia:1311 – 1394, Papers of the British School at Rome, 1966

Maggior Consiglio, Novella, Register 36, folio 419r copia, 1382.

Maggior Consiglio, Register 21,Folio 82v, 1395

Maggior Consiglio Leona, Register 21, folio 112r, folio 230v, 1414.

Maggior Consiglio, Register 23, folio 16v, 1457, folio 145v, 1474, folio 157v, 1476, folio 177v, 1478.

Maggior Consiglio, Register 24, folio 62r, 1485, folio 76r, 1486, folio 187r, 1501.

Mallet, M and Shaw, C; The Italian Wars, 1494 – 1559, Pearson, 2012

Mallett, M: La conquista della Terraferma, Storia di Venezia dalle origini alla caduta della Serenissima, Vol. IV, Il'rinascimento: politica e cultura, Rome: Istituto della Enciclopedia Italiana

Manfroni, C: La battaglia di Gallipoli e la politica veneto-turca (1381-1420), L'Ateneo Veneto, Venice. XXV (II), 1902

Mark, R.F: Venetian Foreign Affairs from 1250 to 1381: The Wars with Genoa and Other External Developments, University of Illinois, 1988

Marsilio (editori): La galea ritrovata Origine delle cose di Venezia, a cura di Consorzio Venezia Nuova, 2002

Maschietto, F. L: Elena Lucrezia Cornaro Piscopia (1646-1684): prima donna laureata nel mondo, Antenore, 1978

Mason, N.D: The War of Candia, 1645-1669, LSU Historical Dissertations and Theses,1972.

Mattingly, G: Renaissance Diplomacy, Cosimo Classics, published 2010.

McClellan, G.B.: Venice and Bonaparte, Literary Licensing LLC, 2011

McEvedy, C. & Jones, R: Atlas of World Population History, Penguin, 1978

Miller, W: The Latins in the Levant: A History of Frankish Greece (1204–1566), John Murray, London, 1908

Miller, W: Essays on the Latin Orient, Cambridge, Cambridge University Press, 1921

Mss, Sivos, Elezioni di Dogi, e Mss, Reggimenti

Montgomery, A. E: The Making of the Treaty of Sèvres of 10 August 1920. The Historical Journal. 15 (4), 1972

Morris, J:The Venetian Empire:A SeaVoyage, Penguine, 1990

Muazzo, G. A: Cronico famiglie nobili Venete andate in Candia, MSS

Murat, J: The Great Extirpation of Hellenism and Christianity in Asia Minor: The Historic and Systematic Deception of World Opinion Concerning the Hideous Christianity's Uprooting of 1922, Miami, 1999

Nani, Storia Veneta, II

Nani, F: Capitolare dei signori di notte, Venezia: Tipografia del tempo, 1877

Nazor, A: Inhabitants of Poljica in the War of Morea (1684–1699), Croatian Institute of History. 21 (21), 2002

Nicol, D. M.: Bizantium and Venice: A study in cultural and deplomatic relations, Cambridge University Press, 1988

Nicol, D.M.: The Reluctant Emperor: A Biography of John Cantacuzene, Byzantine Emperor and Monk, c. 1295-1383, Cambridge University Press, 1996

Nobiltà veneta con le arme et insegne di cadauna famiglia, Volume III, 1725Norwich, J: A History of Venice, Paperback – Illustrated, 1989

Norwich, J: Venice, The Rise to Empire, London, Penguin Books, 1978

Norwich, J: Venice, Byzantium: Decline and Fall, London,Penguin Books, 1995

Palladio; Storia del Friuli, II, 13, Miss

Praga, G: Storia di Dalmazia, Pisa, Giardini, 1993

Queller, E: The Venetian Patriciate: Reality versus Myth, (Chicago: University of Illinois Press, 1986

Rena, L: Venice's Colonial Jews: Community, Identity, and Justice in Late Medieval Venetian Crete, Thesis, Harvard, 2014

Riedmann, J: CAMINO, Rizzardo da, Dizionario Biografico degli Italiani - Volume 17, 1974

Rowland, I: A summer outing in 1510: religion and economics in the papal war with Ferrara, Viator 18, 1987

Rossi, Geovanni, Reggiment e mss, tomo XVIII

Sandi, V,98, Tentori, VIII

Sanuto, Nei Diarii mss, nella marciana, vol III, IV, VII, VIII, X, XXXIII, XXXIV

Sanuto R. I. S. tom xxii

Sassi, F: Le Campagne di Dalmazia durante la Guerra di Candia (1645-1648), Archivio Veneto, 20,1937

Schaller D. J., Zimmerer J: Late Ottoman Genocides – Schaller: The Dissolution of the Ottoman Empire and Young Turkish Population and Extermination Policies. Routledge, 2013

Schönhals, K: Erinnerungen eines österreichischen Veteranen aus dem italienischen Kriege der Jahre 1848 und 1849

Schroder, F, Repertorio Genealogico Delle Famiglie Confermate Nobili e Dei Titolati Nobili, Venice, 1830

Senato Secreta, folio 34v, 1352

Segretario alle Voci, register 1, folio 53v, 1352, folio 59r, 1352 folio 44v, 1352, folio 45r, 1352.
Segretario Voci Register 3, folio 15r, 1387, folio 32v, 1384, folio 1r, 1387.
Segretario Voci Register 4, folio 85r, 1439, folio 100r, 1439, folio 103r, 1340, folio 61r, 1441, folio 105v,1341, folio 103vr, 1341, folio 105v, 1342, folio 108v, 1342, folio 53r, 1443, folio 111r, 1343, folio 86v, 1344, folio 154r, folio 37V, 1444,1445, folio 27r, 1447, folio 117r, 1447, folio 128v, 1450, folio 130r, 1451, folio 134r, 1452, folio 94r, 1453 folio 30r, 1454, folio 30v, 1444, folio 58v, 1447, folio 19v, 1447, folio 122v, 1449, , folio 43v, 1450, folio 86r, 1450, folio 135v, 1453, folio 55r, 1453, folio 54r, 1454, folio 7v, 1458
Segretario Voci Register 5, folio 11v, 1440.
Segretario Voci Register 6, folio 39v, 1471, folio 109r, 1483 folio 78r, 1565, folio 61v, 1570.
Segretario Voci Register 7, folio 0r, 1491, folio 1r, 1499, folio 1v , 1503
Segretario Voci Register 9, folio 3v, 1493, folio 8r, 1495.
Senato Misti, register 25, folio 27r, 1349.
Senato Misti, register 26, folio 24V, 1350.
Senato Misti, register 30, folio 44r, 1361.
Senato Misti, register 31, folio 52v, 1363.
Senato Misti, Register 36, folio 103v, 1380.
Senato Misti, register 37, folio 89r, 1382.
Senato Misti, Register 40, folio 166v, 1389.
Senato Misti, Register 44, folio 128v, 1399.
Setton, K.M: The Papacy and the Levant (1204–1571), Volume III, Philadelphia, The American Philosophical Society, 1984
Setton, K.M: Venice, Austria and the Turks in the 17th Century, American Philosophical Society ,1991
Shahan, T: Aquileia, in Catholic Encyclopidia, Vol 1 Robert Appleton, New York, 1907
Shaw, C: Julius II: The Warrior Pope, Blackwell Publishers, Oxford, 1993

Sivos, Elezioni di Dogi, Mss, Reggimenti
Tabacco, G: Andrea Tron e la crisi dell'aristocrazia senatoria a Venezia, Trieste, Università degli Studi, 1957
Targhetta, R: Leonardo Foscolo, Dizionario Biografico degli Italiani, Volume 49, 1997
Topping, P: Venice's Last Imperial Venture, Proceedings of the American Philosophical Society, 120 (3),1976
Tuohy, T: Herculean Ferrara: Ercole d'este, 1471-1505, and the intervention of a Ducal Capital, Cambridge University Press, 1996
Turkish General Staff, Türk İstiklal Harbinde Batı Cephesi, Edition II, Part 2, Ankara 1999
Turnbull, S: The Ottoman Empire 1326–1699, Essential Histories Series 62, Osprey Publishing, 2003
Vaggassi l'opera: Delle Montete dei Veneziani, Part 1, 1818
Venezia e il Levante (sec XV - sec XVIII), VENIVA consortium, 1996
Verdi iL Libretto Sottoindicato: Pressa di Clissa, 1648
Vincent E.R.P: Ugo Foscolo: An Italian in Regency England, Cambridge, 1953
Von Bode, W: Eine Porträtplakette des Dogen Francesco Foscari von Donatello: Ein Nachtrag, Berliner Museen 45 (2), 1924
Woodhead, C.: The Ottoman World, Routledge Press, 2012

INDEX

Agnadello, Battle of, 58
agnatic-cognatic succession, 116
Andros, Naval Battle of, 97
Armistice of Mudros, 132
Barbaro, Marco Antonio, 68
Baron van Heemstra, 126
Bellegarde, General, 115
Bonaparte, Napoleon, 109
Boniface of Montferrate,, 11
Bragadin, Marco Antonio, 69
Candia Wars of 1545 to 1569, 79
Candian Rebellion, 14
Capra, Enrico, 82
Castle of Monselice, 1
Cavaliere, Marco Zeno, 42
Charles V The Holy Roman Emperor and Archduke of Austria, 64
Charles VII of France, 44
Church of San Marco di Boccalama, 1
Condulmer, Francesco Cardinal, 44
Contarini, Bartolomeo, 97
Cortazzi, Teodoro, Candian Rebellion, 14
Council of Forty (Quarantia), 5
Council of Ten, 5
Council of Wise Men (Consilium Sapientium), 4
Crusade of Varna, 44
Dandalo, Enrico Doge, 11
Dandolo,, 61
Daniel de Hochepieds, 126
Della Bande Nere, 64
Doge, 5
Dolfin, Daniele, 97, 99
Doria, Paganino, Third Venetian Genovese War, 19
Emperor of Constantinople, 22
Erizzo, Francesco Doge, 88
Foscari, Jacopo, 46, 48
Foscolo estate Seydiköy, 126
Foscolo Family
  Aristocratic Titles, 140
  Early Councils of State, 8
  Family Tree, 15
  Heraldry, 142
  Medieval Branch, 11
  Origin, 1
Foscolo, Almorà (1252-1316), 15
Foscolo, Andrea (1314-1363), 15
  Emperor of Constantinople, Case of, 22
  Rizzardo da Camino, Case of, 17
  Third Venetian Genovese

War, 17
Foscolo, Andrea (1363-1438), 36
- *Candian Debt Crisis 1428*, 41
- *Lombardy War 1423*, 41
- *Sultan Mehmed I, Treaty with*, 36

Foscolo, Andrea (1386 - 1458), 44
- *Ambassador to Constantinople*, 44
- *Jacopo Foscarini, pardoning of*, 46
- *Jacopo Foscarini, Trial for Murder*, 46
- *Peace Agreement with Ottomans 1446*, 45
- *Peace Treaty with Ottomans 1454*, 47
- *Treaty of Lodi*, 48

Foscolo, Andrea (1425-1475), 62

Foscolo, Andrea (1450-1528), 55
- *Ambassador to Constantinople*, 57
- *Attempted Alliance With Ottomans*, 60
- *Naval Commander Western Mediterranean*, 56
- *Second Italian War*, 56

Foscolo, Andrea (1470-1528), 63
- *Ambassador to Ferrara*, 63
- *Governor of Crema*, 63
- *Governor of Friuli*, 64

Foscolo, Andrea (1636-1696), Ionian Islands, 107

Foscolo, Andrea (1756-1788), Ionian Islands
- *Farther of Ugo Foscolos*, 107

Foscolo, Daulo August (1785-1860), Archbishop of Corfu, 118

Foscolo, Dom Nico, Middle Ages, 8

Foscolo, Enrico, Candian Branch, 14

Foscolo, Francesco (1330-1393)
- *Ambassador to Constantinople*, 27
- *Argos, Siege of*, 29
- *Marriage of King Peter II of Cyrpus*, 24
- *Padua, Salt Production Dispute*, 23

Foscolo, Francesco (1330-1393), 23

Foscolo, Francesco (1350-1428), 42
- *Governor of Friuli*, 42

Foscolo, Francesco (1604-1664), 93

Foscolo, Francesco (1666 – 1726), 101

Foscolo, Francesco (1739-1793), Agriculturalist, Poet, 103
Foscolo, Francesco (1766-1826), 105
Foscolo, Georgio (Zozi) (1761-1822), 104
Foscolo, Giambattista (1588–1643), 73
Doge of Candia, 73
Foscolo, Giovanni (1739-1800), Levant, 124
Foscolo, Giovanni Battista (1791–1851), 118
Foscolo, Girolamo (1401-1465), 50
Foscolo, Giulio Constantine Angelo
Brother of Ugo Foscolo, 114
Foscolo, Leonardo (1588-1666), 75
Candidacy for Doge, 93
Captain General of the Sea, 90
Early Career, 75
General & Governor of Dalmatia and Albania, 80
Governor of Candia, 77
Later Career, 77
Foscolo, Leonardo (1693-1753), 101
Foscolo, Leonardo (1765-1829), 122
Foscolo, Leonardo Lord of Anafi, 12
Foscolo, Leonardo, and Giovanni Candian Branch, 13
Foscolo, Luigi(1560-1623), 73
Foscolo, Marco (1422-1506), 52
Peace Treaty with Ferrara 1484, 54
Foscolo, Marco (1510-1570, 67
Foscolo, Marco (1579-1630), 73
Foscolo, Marco (1584–1644), 74
Foscolo, Marco (1757-1817), Canon of Padua, 104
Foscolo, Marco, Middle Ages, 8
Foscolo, Michele (1890-1963), 138
Foscolo, Nicholas (1890-1963), 138
Foscolo, Nicolò (1358-1425), 32
Francesco II da Carrara, trial of, 34
Lapanto and Patra, Capture of, 35
Foscolo, Nicolò (1581-1641), 73

Foscolo, Nicolò (1596-1656), Ionian Islands, 107

Foscolo, Nicolò (1670-1703), 96
  Sixth Ottoman Venetian War, 96
Foscolo, Nicolò (1716-1783), Ionian Islands
  Grandfather of Ugo Foscolo, 107
Foscolo, Nicolo (1818-1878), Levant, 124
Foscolo, Paolo (1396-1452), 51
Foscolo, Paolo (1840-1918), Levant, 124
  Aristocratic Title, 127
Foscolo, Pietro (1448-1523), 61
Foscolo, Pietro, Middle Ages, 8
Foscolo, Stefano, Middle Ages, 8
Foscolo, Ugo, Aurelii, 1
Foscolo, Ugo, Poet Italian Nationalist, 109
  Family Origins, 14
  Family Tree, 105
Foscolo, Zaccaria (1468-1540), 65
Foscolo, Zaccaria (1538-1603), 68
Foscolo-Mango Steamship Company, 124

Foscolos, Alfredo (1920-2009), 138
Foscolos, Michail, Dr (1971**),** Notable Academic, Banker, 138
Foscolos, Pavlos, Dr (1924-2017), 138
Foskolos, Hellenised Name, 14
Foskolos, Marco-Antonio (1597 - 1662), 14
Fotiadis family, 124
Fourth Venetian-Genovese War, 25
fourth Venetian-Ottoman War, 67
Francesco Foscolo (1330-1393)
  War of Padua 1387, 26
Francesco I da Carrara, 26
Francesco II da Carrara, 30, 34
Francis I King of France, 63
Gazi Hüseyin Pasha, 88
General Assembly of Men (Conico), 4
Georgio, Caporioni, Candian Rebellion, 14
Ghiara d'Adda, 56
Gil D'As, 82
Golden Book (Libro d'Oro), 9
  Foscolo Family Inclusion, 9
  Registration in, 10
  Under Austrian Rule, 116
Gonzalo de Cordoba, 57

Great Council (Maggior Consiglio), 5
   Foscolo Family Inclusion, 9

   Hereditary Membership, 10
   Lockout (Serrata del Maggior Consiglio), 7
Grimani, Antonio, 56
Gritti, Andrea, 64
Guglielmo della Scala,, 30
Hungarian War 1355, 20
John de lo Cavo, 12
John V, Byzantine Emperor, 27
John VII, Byzantine Emperor, 28
John VIII, Byzantine Emperor, 44
Kapudan Pasha, 92
Kemal, Mustafa, 134
King Lajos of Hungary, 20
King Peter II of Cyprus, 24
King Sigismund of Hungary, 30, 43
Kingdom of Italy, 120
   Nobility, 120
Kingdom of Lombardy-Venezia, 116
   Golden Book, 116
   Nobility, 116
Lemnos, Naval Battle of, 97
Leonardo, and Giovanni Foscolo, 13

Lepanto, battle of, 70
Loredan, Alvise, 44
Louis XII of France, 56, 59, 60
Madonna Lucrezia Borgia, 63
Manin, Ludivico, Doge, 104
   Abdication, 109
Maria of Enghien, 29
Marignano, Battle of, 61
Marin Sanudo, 12
Maximilian Holy Roman Empire and Archduke of Austria, 59
Mehmed IV, 79
Mocenigo, Alvise, 90, 92
Mocenigo, Domenico, 96
Morganatic descendent, 10
Morosini, Francesco, 95
Niccolò III d'Este, 30
Njegovan, Maximilian, Vice-Admiral, 127
Noble Houses
   BrandNew, CasaNovísimas, 9
   New, Case Nuove, 9
   Old, Case Vecchie, 9
Patria del Friuli, 42
Philip of Burgundy, 44
Pisani, Giorgio, 102
Pisani, Nicolo, Third Venetian Genovese War, 19
Pope Alexander, 63
Pope Julius II, 58

Pope Pius V, 70
Pope Pius VII, 118
Renier, Paolo Doge, 102
Ruzzini, Marco, Third Venetian Genovese War, 17
Salic law, 120
Samothrace, Naval Battle of, 98
Senate (Pregardi), 5
Seydiköy, 124
Sforza, Francesco, 45
Signoria, 7
Sixth Ottoman Venetian War (1684-1698), 95
Sultan Bayazid II, 58
Sultan Bayezid, 28
Sultan Mehmed I, 36
Sultan Mehmed II, 45
Sultan Süleyman, 65
Theodore I Palaiologos, 29, 35
Third Ottoman-Venetian War, 65
Third Venetian Genovese War, 17
Treaty of Campoformio, 109
Treaty of Karlowitz, 99
Treaty of Passarowitz, 100
Treaty of Pressburg, 109
Treaty of Sèvres (1920), 134
Tron, Andrea, 102
Valaresso, Zaccaria, 42
Vendramin, Andrea, 80
Venier, Antonio, 47
Viadro, Tommaso, Third Venetian Genovese War, 19
War of Chioggia, 25
  Battles of Anzio and Pola, 25
  Blockade of Chioggia, 25
War of Padua 1402, 30
War of the League of Crambrai, 58
Zeno, Murino, Candian Rebellion, 14

APPENDIX –GENEALOGICAL MANUSCRIPT MARCO BABARO (OUT OF COPYRIGHT)

F. Oscolo

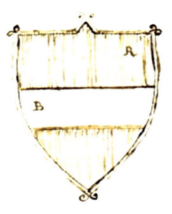

Partirono da monteselice e vennero ad abitar à
matamauco e poi a Rivoalto del 965, et fuore co
minciat la Chiesa di S. Marco in bocca di piaza
dell'orio, qual al presente è rovinata; et altri han
no detto che furono accettati nel gran Consiglio
del 1297 per haverii il doge, e governo de nobili
quando il popolo non volse accetar il dazio della
macina, e si solleuò contro il doge, e erano questi no
bili, che lo haveuano imposto; et altri hanno detto

che furono eletti del gran Consiglio nel senar di
quello: Contro li quali con fu serue li auxoni
nel qui suss.

Vidal Falier Doxe, Pietro Badoer Parnasia di Grado, e nuovi li Vescovi del Dogado, li Giudici, li
nobili Principali, e Popolo di Venetia del 1097 con-
cesero il Castel di Grado alli habitanti di quel per
con obligazione di pagare di pagarsi ogni famiglia ad esso Doxe, vne Galline, e vne denari all'
anno, e di ogni undeci anguille, del pescie
marno uno, e difender li suoi confini dx
gadis. Nominine il Doxe, il Parnasia di Grado
li Giudici, et altri 56, uno delli quali fu Dominici
cus Tusculo

Petrus Tusculus era nominatus al giuramento fes
Domenego Michiel Doxe a quelli de Bari.

Domenego Moroini Doxe con li suoi Giudici, e
Procuratori, e Popolo di Venetia del 1153 fecero
cason di scuverir a Petri, e Zuane Basei delli
danari haueuano hauuto Baselo Basei suo padre, quali spese nel Campanil di s. marco du
prati ue fino alla cima. Nominine il Doxe Dandi

ci, ed altri 299, uno de quali fu marcus Zusto.

Paduano per Colosi in quibus inier Marius Tondo del servior di Castello, Guarardo del servior di S. Crocè, ed Enrico Dou si agnoscki 1452.

Nunciò era del gran Consiglio 1468.

Andrea Tondo fu delli 41 elessero Doxi Pasqual Malipiero 1457.

Andrea di lui figliolo fu delli 41 elessero Doxi Piero Mocenigo 1474, ed Andrea Vendramin 1476.

Andrea di lui figliolo fu delli 41 elessero Doxi Andrea Gritti 1523.

Doxi Marco suo Padre sono li due sudetti, fodelli 41 elessero Doxi Zuane Mocenigo 1478, marco Barbarigo 1485, Agostin Barbarigo 1486, e Lorando Loredan 1501.

Andrea Tondo fodelli 41 elessero Doxi Enrico Dandolo 1192.

Per li quali nuovamenti appare, che erano al Governo inanzi il 1297, ma può esser, che fu-
ino di questa Famiglia non sia eletto in quel
tempo del gran Consiglio per' qualche cagione.

Inanzi il serar del gran Consiglio 1297 erano
di quello gl' infrascritti, nelli anni infrascritti.

Chierico Michiel 1261
Filippo Michiel 1279, 1281, 1285, uno del
1280.
Del 1285 fu Vicedomino del suo.

Del 1288 sopra gl' impresidi, p Filippo Michiel, e
Marco Michiel, e p Pietro Miani.

        Del sestier di S. Croce
1264, 1285 Michiel Michiel

        Del sestier di Cannareggio
1266, 1276, 1277 fl Iaco Michiel

                                  Paolo

Paulo Tiepolo q. Andrea prese il suo cognome con
Caterina Sandelli 1519. —

           in uno manoscritto ho letto così.
Tiepolo nominato dalli figli. Furono huomini molto
semplici, ma molto favoriti dalla fortuna, si che
tosto ricchi furono altresi anch'essi del maggior
consiglio al tempo del serrar di quello inq̃s.
Furono edificatori di s. marco Boccalaro.

in altro nessuno anco ho trovato.
Emilia Venerio da Gedi. sono Tribuni antiqui et
gran huomini del nostro.

Almáro Toodo
                Johannes
   Marcus   Andreas
Nagyberi Andreas Nicolai
Paulines Nicolai Andreas
Aluisi Andreas Rex Andreas Nadai
            Zacharia   Andreas
            Nicolai   Nicolai
         Zacharia Franciscus
           Aluise Andreas Nicolai Johannes Zacharia
         Zacharia Gerardo, Andreas Nicolai Andreas Johannes

Made in the USA
Middletown, DE
30 July 2024